★ American Girl®

Summer Treats

Photography **Nicole Hill Gerulat**

weldon**owen**

Contents

Summer Fun for Everyone!

From ice pops and sundaes to seasonal cakes and pies, the summer months hold the promise of cooling treats, icy drinks, and sweet desserts that make the most of the warm weather and the season's fresh fruits. Surprise your friends with a fruity coffeecake the morning after a sleepover, enjoy a fizzy ice cream float next to the pool, or cool down with a chocolaty sundae after a day in the sun. The more than fifty recipes in these pages will give you loads of ideas about the very best ways to stay cool when the days and nights get hot.

You'll learn how to whip up ice cream from scratch, layer and swirl ice pops with colorful panache, bake and decorate cakes and cupcakes like a pro, and make the perfect crust for a fruit pie. Easy-to-follow instructions plus helpful tips and simple techniques will ensure your success with every recipe. Check out our list of the important tools you'll need, then flip through these pages for inspiration before you get started. Most recipes include options for serving and varying ingredients, so feel free to change things up as you wish and let your creativity flow!

If staying cool is your No. 1 priority, try Mermaid Pops (page 91) and easy Fruit Slushies (page 107). For snacks that are simple to transport to the pool or a picnic, make Strawberry Hand Pies (page 80) and Pineapple Cupcakes (page 42). To show off the season's fresh fruit, go for Peach Pie (page 61) or Blackberry Tart (page 78). And when it's time to celebrate the Fourth of July, check out the Red, White & Blueberry Cake (page 21) and the Fireworks Bundt Cake (page 23) for colorful and scrumptious sweet treats to celebrate the occasion.

Cool Tips

★ KEEP PASTRY COLD ★

Pie and tart dough should be kept cold to ensure the flakiest pastry, so chill the dough well before rolling it out and refrigerate or briefly freeze the pastry-lined pans before baking. If the dough becomes too soft to manage, wrap it in plastic wrap and refrigerate until it's firm enough to handle.

★ PIPE GLAZE LIKE A PRO ★

Glazing cookies is easier than you might think. To fill the piping bag with ease, place it tip-end down in a tall glass, then fold the open end over the glass rim to hold it open. First pipe the glaze around the perimeter of the cookie, then add more icing to the center. Give the glazed cookie a gentle shake to "flood" the icing to the edge, coating the cookie evenly.

★ FREEZE ICE CREAM ★

Refrigerate ice cream and sorbet mixtures until very cold before transferring them to an ice cream maker. Mixtures that are not sufficiently chilled may not freeze properly during processing.

★ MAKE ICE POPS ★

No ice pop molds? No problem! Use small paper or plastic cups instead, inserting an ice pop stick into the cup once the mixture has partially frozen. To unmold the pops easily, run the bottoms of the cups under hot water.

The tools you'll need

★ **Measuring cups and spoons** help you measure ingredients accurately and easily. Choose graduated sets for dry ingredients and a glass measuring cup for liquids.

★ **An electric mixer** is handy for making batters and frostings and whipping cream.

★ **Oven mitts or pads** protect your hands from hot pans, cookie sheets, and oven racks.

★ **An ice cream scoop** is helpful for scooping ice cream and dividing batter evenly into muffin pans.

★ **Baking pans and dishes** are used for baking all kinds of batters and doughs. The essential ones are a 9-by-13-inch pan, a 10-inch Bundt pan, round and square cake pans, pie dishes, muffin pans, and ramekins.

★ **Small metal icing spatulas** are good for spreading frosting on cupcakes and cakes.

★ **Rimmed cookie sheets**, especially thick ones, are useful for toasting coconut and transporting cupcakes while they are cooling.

★ **A piping bag** fitted with a plain or star-shaped tip is a good way to frost cupcakes and glaze cookies. If you don't have one, a zippered plastic bag with a corner snipped off works well.

★ **An ice cream maker** churns ice cream and sorbet mixtures into delicious frozen treats.

★ **Ice pop molds** will help freeze mixtures into grab-and-go snacks.

★ **Parchment paper** is used to line cookie sheets and pans so that baked goods won't stick.

Cooking with care

Adults have lots of culinary wisdom and can help keep you safe in the kitchen. Always have an adult assist you, especially if your recipe involves high heat, hot ovens, sharp objects, and electric appliances.

 This symbol appears throughout the book to remind you that you'll need an adult to help you with all or part of the recipe. Ask for help before continuing.

Whether you're baking cookies and cupcakes for a beach picnic or preparing ice cream cake for a special occasion, cooling summer desserts are a yummy seasonal treat.

Make it special

★ Make a big impression by going the extra mile when embellishing your treats. Decorate cupcakes with fresh flowers, drizzle chocolate sauce over a sundae, or simply add a paper umbrella to a fruit slushie or ice cream float. These little touches will go a long way toward making your summertime goodies memorable!

★ Frozen citrus cups make cool and colorful bowls for serving ice cream and sorbet. To make them, cut an orange, lemon, or grapefruit in half crosswise. Use a grapefruit knife to cut around the flesh and remove it, then scrape out any remaining pulp with the tip of a spoon. Freeze the shells until solid, about 1 hour, then fill them with your favorite frozen treat.

★ Give plain ice cream shakes some pizzazz by adding whipped cream and sprinkles. You can also dip glass rims in melted chocolate (see page 89 for the technique), then in shredded dried coconut or sprinkles. If your shake is a fruity one, try pressing cut fresh fruit against the side of the glass (page 89) before filling it.

★ Ice cream is always delicious, but even better when sandwiched between palm-sized cookies (page 104) or scooped into small balls and cloaked in melted chocolate and sprinkles (page 97). You can also try giving plain ice cream cones a boost by dipping them in melted chocolate, then in chopped nuts or candies before adding a scoop.

Cakes, Cupcakes & Cookies

Watermelon Cake

A watermelon cake that tastes just like strawberries? Yes, please!
Much of the vibrant red coloring for this playful, summertime cake
comes from crushed, freeze-dried strawberries in the batter.

MAKES 8 TO 10 SERVINGS

CAKE

Nonstick cooking spray

1 cup freeze-dried
strawberries

2 cups all-purpose flour

½ teaspoon salt

12 tablespoons (1½ sticks)
unsalted butter, at room
temperature

1½ cups granulated sugar

3 large eggs

2 teaspoons vanilla extract

2 tablespoons red
food coloring, plus more
as needed

1 cup buttermilk

1½ teaspoons baking soda

1 teaspoon white vinegar

¾ cup mini semisweet
chocolate chips

Preheat the oven to 350°F. Trace the bottom of two 9-inch round cake pans onto sheets of parchment paper and cut out the circles with scissors. Spray the bottom of the pans with nonstick cooking spray. Put the paper circles in the pans. Spray the paper and the sides of the pans.

Place the freeze-dried strawberries in a zippered plastic bag and seal shut. Using a rolling pin, roll over the strawberries in the bag to form a fine powder.

In a medium bowl, whisk together the flour, salt, and strawberry powder. In a large bowl, using an electric mixer, beat the butter and granulated sugar on medium speed until light and fluffy, 2 to 3 minutes. Add the eggs one at a time, beating well after each addition. Add the vanilla and red food coloring and beat until combined. Add more food coloring if needed until the desired color is reached. Turn off the mixer and add about half of the flour mixture. Mix on low speed just until blended. Pour in the buttermilk and mix just until combined. Add the remaining flour mixture and mix just until blended. Turn off the mixer and scrape down the bowl with a rubber spatula. In a small bowl, stir together the baking soda and vinegar, then quickly add the mixture to the batter and stir until combined. Stir in the chocolate chips.

Divide the batter evenly between the prepared cake pans and spread in an even layer. Bake until a wooden skewer inserted into the center of the cakes comes out clean, 25 to 30 minutes. Using oven mitts, remove the pans from the oven and set them on wire racks. Let cool for 10 minutes, then run a knife

~ Continued on page 20 ~

No seeds!

Mini chocolate chips added to the batter melt ever so slightly during baking. If you prefer your cake "seedless," just leave them out.

VANILLA FROSTING

1 cup (2 sticks) unsalted butter, at room temperature

5 cups powdered sugar

6 tablespoons whole milk

2 teaspoons vanilla extract

¼ teaspoon salt

Red and green food coloring

1 tablespoon bittersweet chocolate chips

~ Continued from page 19 ~

around the inside edge of each pan. Turn the pans over onto the racks. Lift off the pans, remove the parchment paper, and let the cakes cool completely, about 1 hour.

Meanwhile, make the frosting: In a large bowl, using an electric mixer, beat the butter on medium speed until light and fluffy, about 2 minutes. Add the powdered sugar, milk, vanilla, and salt and beat on low speed just until combined. Turn off the mixer and scrape down the bowl. Beat on medium-high speed until the frosting is airy and smooth, about 5 minutes.

To decorate the cake, scoop about ½ of the frosting into a small bowl, add 5 drops of red food coloring, and stir to combine. Stir in more coloring until the shade of red matches the cake. Scoop the remaining frosting into another bowl. Add 5 drops of green food coloring and stir to combine. Stir in more coloring until the frosting is the dark green color of a watermelon rind.

Place 1 cake layer, bottom side down, on a cake plate. Spread half of the red frosting on top of the cake, smoothing it with an icing spatula. Place the other cake layer, bottom side up, on top. Spread the remaining red frosting on top of the cake, leaving 1 inch around the edge of the cake uncovered. Spread the green frosting over the cake sides and around the top edge of the cake, stopping at the red frosting. Arrange the chocolate chips over the red frosting to look like watermelon seeds. Cut the cake into slices and serve.

Red, White & Blueberry Cake

Perfect for your July 4th celebration, this tender vanilla cake is topped with fresh fruit arranged in the design of an American flag. With broad stripes of raspberries and white icing and bright stars of blueberries, the festive cake is a fun and patriotic summer treat.

MAKES 10 TO 12 SERVINGS

3 cups all-purpose flour, plus flour for dusting

2 teaspoons baking powder

¾ teaspoon baking soda

¾ teaspoon salt

1 cup (2 sticks) unsalted butter, at room temperature, plus butter for greasing

2 cups sugar

2 large eggs plus 2 large egg yolks

1 tablespoon vanilla extract

2 cups buttermilk

Vanilla Frosting, store-bought or homemade (page 20; omit food coloring)

1 cup blueberries

4 cups raspberries

Preheat the oven to 350°F. Butter a 9-by-13-inch baking pan, line the bottom of the pan with parchment paper, then butter the parchment. Dust with flour, then tap out the excess.

Sift together the flour, baking powder, baking soda, and salt into a medium bowl. In a large bowl, using an electric mixer, beat the butter and sugar on medium speed until light and fluffy, about 2 minutes. Add the eggs and the egg yolks one at a time, beating well after each addition. Beat in the vanilla. Turn off the mixer and scrape down the bowl with a rubber spatula. With the mixer on low speed, beat in the flour mixture in three additions, alternating with the buttermilk in two additions, beginning and ending with the the flour and beating just until blended after each addition. Turn off the mixer and scrape down the bowl. Raise the speed to high and beat for 20 seconds.

Pour the batter into the prepared pan. Bake until a wooden skewer inserted into the center of the cake comes out clean, about 55 minutes. Using oven mitts, remove the pan from the oven and set it on a wire rack. Let cool for 10 minutes, then run a table knife around the inside edge of the pan. Turn the pan over onto the racks. Lift off the pan and peel off the parchment. Let cool.

Prepare the frosting. Spread the frosting evenly over the top and sides of the cake. Using the blueberries and raspberries, create the colors of the American flag, with the blueberries arranged in a square in the top-left corner of the cake and the raspberries arranged in thick horizontal stripes across the top of the cake. Cut the cake into pieces and serve.

Fireworks Bundt Cake

Watch your friends' faces as you cut this dessert to reveal bright splashes of red and blue cake — they're sure to be surprised! Take care not to mix the colored batters together too much or your creation will end up with splotches of purple.

MAKES 10 TO 12 SERVINGS

CAKE

3 cups cake flour, plus flour for dusting

¼ teaspoon baking soda

¼ teaspoon salt

1 cup (2 sticks) unsalted butter, at room temperature, plus butter for greasing

2½ cups granulated sugar

6 large eggs, at room temperature

2 teaspoons vanilla extract

1 cup sour cream

Red and blue food coloring

To make the cake, preheat the oven to 325°F. Butter a 10-inch Bundt pan. Dust with flour, then tap out the excess.

In a medium bowl, stir together the flour, baking soda, and salt. In a large bowl, using an electric mixer, beat the butter and sugar on medium-high speed until light and fluffy, 5 to 7 minutes. Turn off the mixer and scrape down the bowl with a rubber spatula. Add the eggs one at a time, beating on medium-high speed until blended after each addition. Add the vanilla and beat until blended. Turn off the mixer and add about one-third of the flour mixture. Mix on low speed just until blended. Add about half of the sour cream and mix just until combined. Add about half of the remaining flour mixture and mix just until blended. Add the remaining sour cream and mix just until combined. Add the remaining flour mixture and mix just until blended. Turn off the mixer and scrape down the bowl.

Scoop a heaping 1 cup of the batter into a small bowl. Scoop another heaping 1 cup of the batter into another small bowl. Transfer the remaining batter to the prepared pan, spreading it evenly. Add 8 drops of red food coloring to the batter in one small bowl and gently fold it in. Then add 8 drops of blue food coloring to the batter in the other small bowl and gently fold it in. Spoon the red batter in blobs over the plain batter in the pan, then spoon the blue batter in blobs between the red batter blobs. Draw a wooden skewer or a chopstick through the batter in a series of figure eights to create a marbled effect.

~ Continued on page 24 ~

Star bright

Edible silver stars make a festive finishing touch. If unavailable, try red, blue, or plain sugar sprinkles instead.

~ Continued from page 23 ~

Bake until a wooden skewer inserted near the center of the cake comes out clean, 1¼ to 1½ hours. Using oven mitts, remove the pan from the oven and set it on a wire rack. Let cool for 10 minutes, then turn the pan over onto the rack, lift off the pan, and let the cake cool completely.

VANILLA ICING

2 cups powdered sugar, sifted

3 tablespoons whole milk, or as needed

1 teaspoon vanilla extract

Red and blue food coloring

Silver star sprinkles for decorating

Meanwhile, make the icing: In a medium bowl, stir together the powdered sugar, milk, and vanilla until smooth, adding a few more drops of milk if needed for the best consistency. Spoon one third of the icing into a small bowl, and another third of the icing into another small bowl. Add 4 or 5 drops of red food coloring to the icing in one bowl and stir until blended. Add 4 or 5 drops of blue food coloring to the icing in the other bowl and stir until blended. Working with one color icing at a time, drizzle the icing over the cake so it runs down the sides. Scatter star sprinkles on top. Cut the cake into slices and serve.

Mixed Berry Shortcake

If you have any leftover shortcakes and berries, make a delicious sundae the next day. Crumble the shortcakes into an ice cream glass, top with a scoop of vanilla or strawberry ice cream and the extra berries, and finish with a dollop of whipped cream. Then dig in!

MAKES 6 SERVINGS

**2 cups all-purpose flour,
plus flour for dusting**

**¼ cup plus 1 to
2 tablespoons
granulated sugar**

2 teaspoons baking powder

¼ teaspoon salt

**6 tablespoons (¾ stick)
cold unsalted butter,
cut into small cubes**

¾ cup heavy cream

**2 cups mixed berries,
such as raspberries
and strawberries**

WHIPPED CREAM

1 cup heavy cream

**1 tablespoon
granulated sugar**

1 teaspoon vanilla extract

**Powdered sugar
for dusting**

Preheat the oven to 375°F. Line a cookie sheet with parchment paper.

In a large bowl, whisk together the flour, the ¼ cup granulated sugar, the baking powder, and salt. Add the butter and, using a pastry blender or 2 knives, make quick, firm chopping motions to cut the butter into the flour mixture until it looks like coarse crumbs, with some chunks the size of peas. Add the cream and stir until the dough starts to come together.

Sprinkle a work surface with flour. Dump the dough onto the floured surface and pat it into a disk. Using a rolling pin, roll out the dough, giving the disk a quarter turn now and then, into a round slab that's 1 inch thick. Pat the sides to make them neat.

Using a 3-inch biscuit cutter, cut out 4 rounds. Gather the dough scraps, roll them out again, and cut out 2 more rounds.

Transfer the dough rounds to the prepared cookie sheet, spacing them evenly apart. Bake until the shortcakes are golden brown on top, 18 to 20 minutes. Using oven mitts, remove the cookie sheet from the oven and set it on a wire rack. Let the shortcakes cool for 10 to 15 minutes.

~ Continued on page 28 ~

Fruity twist

Sub in any of your favorite summer fruits for the berries. Try sliced peaches, nectarines, plums, pluots, or cherries, selecting the best seasonal fruit.

~ *Continued from page 26* ~

Meanwhile, put the strawberries on a cutting board. Pull or cut out the stem and white core from the center of each strawberry, then cut them into thin slices. Put all of the berries in a medium bowl and sprinkle with the remaining 1 to 2 tablespoons granulated sugar (the amount depends on how sweet the berries are—taste one!). Let the berries stand for 10 minutes.

In a large bowl, using an electric mixer, beat the cream, granulated sugar, and vanilla on low speed until the cream begins to thicken and no longer splatters, about 2 minutes. Raise the speed to medium-high and beat until the cream forms soft peaks that fall to one side when the beaters are lifted (turn off the mixer first!), about 3 minutes.

Cut each cooled shortcake in half horizontally. Place the shortcake bottoms, cut side up, on serving plates and spoon the berries on top, dividing them equally. Add a big spoonful of whipped cream and top with the shortcake tops. Put the powdered sugar in a fine-mesh sieve, hold it over the shortcakes, and tap the side to dust the shortcakes with an even layer of the sugar. Serve right away.

Lemon-Blackberry Crumb Bars

The double dose of lemon juice and zest in the cake batter really brings out the flavor of the berries. You could swap in blueberries or raspberries for the blackberries, or use any combo of the three. Be sure to zest the lemon before you juice it.

MAKES ABOUT 18 BARS

TOPPING

¾ cup all-purpose flour

⅓ cup firmly packed light brown sugar

¼ cup granulated sugar

1 teaspoon ground cinnamon

½ cup (1 stick) cold unsalted butter

CAKE

1½ cups all-purpose flour

¾ cup granulated sugar

1½ teaspoons baking powder

½ teaspoon salt

4 tablespoons (½ stick) unsalted butter

1 large egg

½ cup whole milk

1 teaspoon vanilla extract

Zest and juice of 1 lemon

5 cups blackberries

¼ cup granulated sugar

Preheat the oven to 350°F. Butter a 9-by-13-inch metal or glass baking pan.

To make the topping, in a medium bowl, mix the flour, both sugars, and cinnamon. Cut the butter into ½-inch pieces and, using a fork or your hands, rub the butter into the flour mixture until coarse crumbs form. Set aside.

To make the cake, in a medium bowl, whisk together the flour, granulated sugar, baking powder, and salt. Cut the butter into chunks, place it in a microwave-safe bowl, and microwave on high until melted, about 20 seconds. In a large bowl, using an electric mixer, beat the egg, melted butter, milk, vanilla, and lemon zest and juice on medium speed until creamy, about 1 minute. Turn off the mixer and scrape down the bowl with a rubber spatula. Add the flour mixture and beat on low speed just until combined. Turn off the mixer and scrape down the bowl. Pour the batter into the prepared pan.

In a medium bowl, toss together the blackberries and granulated sugar. Scatter the berries on top of the cake batter. Sprinkle the topping evenly over the berries.

Bake until the cake is golden brown and a wooden skewer inserted into the center comes out clean, 35 to 40 minutes. Using oven mitts, remove the pan from the oven and set it on a wire rack. Let cool for at least 20 minutes. Cut the cake into bars and serve.

Flower Cookie Pops

Use icing in a variety of different hues to make a garden's worth of summery cookie pops. Arrange the pops on the cookie sheet with the sticks pointing towards the pan center to prevent the sticks from browning during baking.

MAKES ABOUT 20 COOKIE POPS

3 cups all-purpose flour

1 teaspoon baking powder

½ teaspoon salt

1 cup (2 sticks) unsalted butter, at room temperature

1¼ cups sugar

1 large egg

2 teaspoons vanilla extract

1 tablespoon heavy cream

In a medium bowl, whisk together the flour, baking powder, and salt. In a large bowl, using an electric mixer, beat the butter and sugar on medium-high speed until light and fluffy, 2 to 3 minutes. Add the egg and vanilla and beat on low speed until well combined. Add the flour mixture in three batches, mixing on low speed after each addition, until the flour is almost blended in. Turn off the mixer and scrape down the bowl with a rubber spatula. Add the cream and beat on low speed just until combined.

Scrape the dough onto a piece of plastic wrap, cover it with the wrap, and shape it into a disc. Refrigerate until firm, at least 1 hour or up to overnight.

Preheat the oven to 350°F. Line 2 cookie sheets with parchment paper. Lightly dust your work surface with flour, unwrap the dough, and set it on the surface. If the dough is too hard to roll directly from the refrigerator, let it stand at room temperature for a few minutes. Dust your rolling pin with flour and roll out the dough to an even ⅜-inch thickness.

Using a 3-inch flower-shaped cookie cutter, cut out shapes from the dough. With a metal spatula, carefully move the cutouts to the prepared cookie sheets, arranging them 3 across and 4 down around the perimeter of the pan and spacing them about 1 inch apart. Gather the dough scraps and press them together, then roll them out and cut out additional shapes. Gently insert an ice pop stick into the side of each cookie, pointing the sticks towards the center of the pan to prevent burning.

~ *Continued on page 32* ~

~ Continued from page 31 ~

ROYAL ICING

4 cups powdered sugar

3 tablespoons meringue powder

½ cup warm water, plus more as needed

½ teaspoon vanilla extract or ¼ teaspoon almond extract (optional)

Food coloring of your choice

Rainbow sprinkles, sanding sugar, or other decorations of your choice

20 wooden ice pop sticks

Bake 1 cookie sheet at a time until the edges of the cookies are light golden brown, 14 to 16 minutes. Remove the sheet from the oven and set it on a wire rack. Let cool for 5 minutes, then use the metal spatula to move the cookies directly to the rack. Repeat to bake the rest of the cookies. Let cool completely.

Meanwhile, make the royal icing: In a large bowl, using an electric mixer, beat the sugar, meringue powder, ½ cup warm water, and vanilla (if using) on medium speed until the mixture is very thick but drizzleable, 7 to 8 minutes.

Divide the icing among small bowls, using one bowl for each color. Stir 2 to 3 drops of food coloring into each bowl. Spoon each color of icing into a pastry bag with a plain tip or a lock-top plastic bag with a corner snipped.

Pipe icing around the edge of a cookie to form a border, then pipe icing—the same color or a different one—into the center of the cookie, letting it run to the border. Gently tap the cookie against the work surface a couple of times to get the icing to settle into a smooth, even layer, then sprinkle with sanding sugar or sprinkles. Repeat with the remaining cookies and icing.

Let the icing on the cookies dry at room temperature until firm, at least 6 hours or up to overnight. (To store the cookies, layer them between pieces of parchment paper in an airtight container. They will keep for up to 3 days at room temperature.)

Plum Upside-Down Cake

Upside-down cakes emerge from the oven looking quite plain, until they are unmolded to reveal the lovely caramelized fruit. To make sure that step goes smoothly, run a knife around the inside edge of the pan before inverting it, then let the cake release naturally.

MAKES 8 TO 10 SERVINGS

3 Tbsp plus ½ cup unsalted butter, at room temperature

¾ cup firmly packed light brown sugar

5 or 6 ripe but firm plums such as Santa Rosa, about 1½ lb total weight, halved, pitted, and quartered

1⅓ cups cake flour

1½ teaspoons baking powder

¼ teaspoon salt

¾ cup granulated sugar

2 large eggs

1 teaspoon vanilla extract

⅔ cup buttermilk

Vanilla ice cream for serving

In a 10-inch ovenproof frying pan (preferably cast iron) over medium heat, melt the 3 tablespoons butter. Add the brown sugar and cook, stirring, until the sugar melts and bubbles, about 4 minutes. Let cool slightly. Carefully arrange the plum quarters in the pan in concentric circles.

Preheat the oven to 375°F. In a bowl, sift together the flour, baking powder, and salt. In the bowl of an electric mixer fitted with the paddle attachment, beat the ½ cup butter and the granulated sugar on medium-high speed until light and fluffy, 2 to 3 minutes. Add the eggs one at a time, beating well after each addition. Beat in the vanilla. On low speed, stir in half of the flour mixture, then the buttermilk and the remaining flour mixture, beating just until combined.

Dollop the batter over the fruit and smooth as evenly as you can. Bake until a toothpick inserted into the center of the cake comes out clean, about 40 minutes. Using oven mitts, remove the cake from the oven and set it on a wire rack. Let cool for about 15 minutes. Place a serving plate, upside down, over the pan. Using the oven mitts, carefully invert the plate and pan together, then lift off the pan. Cut the cake into wedges and serve with big scoops of vanilla ice cream.

Day at the Beach Cupcakes

On those summer days when you can't make it to the beach, these yummy cupcakes are the next best thing. Blue frosting is swirled to resemble ocean waves, and crushed vanilla cookies look like sand. A paper umbrella lends the finishing touch.

MAKES 12 CUPCAKES

1¼ cups all-purpose flour

1¼ teaspoons baking powder

¼ teaspoon salt

6 tablespoons (¾ stick) unsalted butter, at room temperature

¾ cup sugar

2 large eggs

1 teaspoon vanilla extract

⅓ cup whole milk

Blue food coloring

1 cup plain vanilla cookies, such as Nilla wafers

1½ cups store-bought vanilla frosting or 1 recipe Coconut–Cream Cheese Frosting (page 43)

12 paper umbrellas

 Preheat the oven to 350°F. Line a 12-cup muffin pan with paper liners.

In a medium bowl, whisk together the flour, baking powder, and salt. In a large bowl, using an electric mixer, beat the butter and sugar on medium-high speed until light and fluffy, 2 to 3 minutes. Add the eggs one at a time, beating well after each addition. Beat in the vanilla. Turn off the mixer and scrape down the bowl. Add about half of the flour mixture and beat on low speed just until blended. Beat in the milk and a few drops of blue food coloring. Add the remaining flour mixture and beat just until blended.

Divide the batter evenly among the prepared muffin cups. Bake until the tops are light golden brown and a wooden skewer inserted into the center of a cupcake comes out clean, 18 to 20 minutes. Using oven mitts, remove the pan from the oven and set it on a wire rack. Let the cupcakes cool in the pan for 10 minutes, then transfer them directly to the rack. Let cool completely.

Meanwhile, place the cookies in a zippered plastic bag. Using a rolling pin, roll over the cookies in the bag until finely ground. Transfer the crumbs to a plate.

Prepare the frosting. Using a small spatula, cover half of each cupcake with some frosting, then dip the frosted cupcake into the cookie crumbs. Add 5 or 6 drops of blue food coloring to the remaining frosting in the bowl and stir briefly. Top the remaining half of each cupcake with the blue frosting. Place a paper umbrella into the "sand" on each cupcake and serve.

Sand Dollar Snickerdoodles

These buttery discs look just like the sandy treasures you might discover while beachcombing along the coast. Pack them in an airtight container for a seaside picnic, or serve them at home to create a beachy mood no matter how far you live from the ocean.

MAKES ABOUT 36 COOKIES

2¾ cups all-purpose flour

1 teaspoon baking powder

1 teaspoon salt

1 cup (2 sticks) unsalted butter, at room temperature

1¾ cups granulated sugar

2 large eggs

2 teaspoons vanilla extract

1 teaspoon ground cinnamon

1 cup sliced almonds

White sanding sugar or turbinado sugar for sprinkling

In a medium bowl, whisk together the flour, baking powder, and salt. In a large bowl, using an electric mixer, beat the butter and 1½ cups of the granulated sugar on medium speed until well blended, about 1 minute. Add the eggs one at a time, beating well after each addition. Beat in the vanilla. Gradually beat in the flour on low speed just until blended. Turn off the mixer and scrape down the bowl.

Transfer the dough to the center of a large piece of plastic wrap. Cover the dough with the plastic wrap and shape into a log about 2 inches in diameter. Refrigerate for 30 minutes or for up to 1 day.

Peheat the oven to 350°F. Line 2 cookie sheets with parchment paper.

In a small bowl, stir together the remaining ¼ cup granulated sugar and the cinnamon. Pour the cinnamon-sugar onto a plate.

Remove the dough log from the refrigerator and remove the plastic wrap. Roll the dough in the cinnamon sugar, coating the entire surface. Cut the dough into ¼-inch slices. Transfer to the prepared cookie sheets, spacing the cookies about 2 inches apart. In the center of each cookie, arrange 5 almond slices in a circle to create a sand dollar design. Sprinkle the cookies with sanding sugar.

Bake 1 cookie sheet at a time until the cookies are lightly browned at the edges, about 10 minutes. Using oven mitts, remove the cookie sheet from the oven and set it on a wire rack. Let cool for 5 minutes, then move the cookies directly to the rack. Repeat to bake the rest of the cookies. Let cool completely.

Bake it fresh
Make the dough for these easy refrigerator cookies in advance, then cut and bake them when you're ready for something sweet.

Chewy Oatmeal Cookies

Remove these palm-size cookies from the oven when the edges are just starting to brown for the perfect chewy consistency. Store any leftovers in an airtight container at room temperature for up to 5 days.

MAKES ABOUT 30 COOKIES

1½ cups all-purpose flour

2 teaspoons ground cinnamon

1 teaspoon baking soda

½ teaspoon salt

12 tablespoons (1½ sticks) unsalted butter, at room temperature

1 cup firmly packed light brown sugar

½ cup granulated sugar

2 large eggs

2 teaspoons vanilla extract

2¼ cups old-fashioned oats

1 cup golden or black raisins, dried currants, or chocolate chips (optional)

 Position 2 racks in the oven so that they are evenly spaced and preheat the oven to 350°F. Line 2 cookie sheets with parchment paper.

Sift together the flour, cinnamon, baking soda, and salt into a medium bowl. In a large bowl, using an electric mixer, beat the butter and both sugars on medium-high speed until combined. Add the eggs 1 at a time, beating well after each addition. Add the vanilla and beat until blended. Turn off the mixer and add the flour mixture and oats. Mix on low speed just until blended. Using the spatula or a wooden spoon, gently stir in the raisins (if using).

Scoop up a rounded tablespoonful of dough, then use your finger to push the dough onto 1 of the prepared cookie sheets. Repeat with the rest of the dough, spacing the mounds well apart.

Bake until the cookies are golden brown, about 15 minutes, rotating the cookie sheets about halfway through baking (ask an adult for help). Using oven mitts, remove the cookie sheets from the oven and set them on wire racks. Let cool for 5 minutes, then use a metal spatula to move the cookies directly to the racks. Let cool completely.

Chocolate Crinkle Cookies

With a crispy, crackled exterior and a chewy, fudgy interior, these cookies satisfy multiple chocolate cravings. Rolling the dough in powdered sugar will reveal the cracks when the cookies bake, or leave them plain for a pure chocolate exterior.

MAKES ABOUT 30 COOKIES

4 ounces unsweetened chocolate, chopped

4 tablespoons (½ stick) unsalted butter

1½ cups all-purpose flour

½ cup Dutch-process cocoa powder

2 teaspoons baking powder

¼ teaspoon salt

4 large eggs

2 cups granulated sugar

1 teaspoon vanilla extract

1½ cups miniature semisweet chocolate chips

½ cup powdered sugar (optional)

In a microwave-safe bowl, combine the chocolate and butter. Microwave on high power, stirring every 20 seconds, just until the mixture is melted and smooth. Let cool for 5 to 7 minutes.

In a medium bowl, whisk together the flour, cocoa powder, baking powder, and salt. Set aside.

In a large bowl, combine the eggs, granulated sugar, and vanilla. Using a wire whisk or an electric mixer on medium speed, beat until light in color and thick, about 3 minutes. Stir in the melted chocolate mixture or beat on low speed until blended. Add the flour mixture and stir or beat until incorporated. Stir or beat in the chocolate chips. Cover the bowl with plastic wrap and refrigerate until the dough is firm enough to roll into balls, about 2 hours.

Preheat the oven to 325°F. Line 2 cookie sheets with parchment paper.

If using powdered sugar, sift it into a small bowl. Scoop up a rounded tablespoonful of dough and roll it into a 1½-inch ball. Coat the ball in the powdered sugar (if using). Place the dough ball on the prepared cookie sheets. Repeat with the rest of the dough, spacing the cookies about 3 inches apart.

Bake until the tops of the cookies are puffed and crinkled and feel firm when lightly touched, 13 to 17 minutes, rotating the sheets about halfway through baking (ask an adult for help). Using oven mitts, remove the cookie sheets from the oven and set them on a wire rack. Let cool for 5 minutes, then use a metal spatula to move the cookies directly to the rack. Let cool completely.

Pineapple Cupcakes

The combination of pineapple and coconut is terrifically tropical. Pineapple juice and crushed pineapple in the batter make these cupcakes very moist, and adding coconut extract to the tangy cream cheese frosting is the secret to their irresistible flavor.

MAKES 16 CUPCAKES

1 cups all-purpose flour

1 cup sweetened shredded coconut, toasted

1¼ teaspoons baking powder

¼ teaspoon salt

1 (8-ounce) can crushed pineapple, drained, juice reserved

½ cup canned coconut milk

½ cup (1 stick) unsalted butter, at room temperature

¾ cup plus 2 tablespoons sugar

1 large egg plus 1 large egg white

1 teaspoon vanilla extract

 Preheat the oven to 350°F. Line 16 cups (of two 12-cup muffin pans) with paper or foil liners.

In a medium bowl, whisk together the flour, coconut, baking powder, and salt. In a liquid measuring cup, stir together ½ cup of the reserved pineapple juice and the coconut milk.

In a large bowl, using an electric mixer, beat the butter and sugar on medium-high speed until light and fluffy, 2 to 3 minutes. Turn off the mixer and scrape down the bowl with a rubber spatula. Add the egg and beat on medium-high speed until blended. Add the egg white and beat until blended. Turn off the mixer and scrape down the bowl. Add the vanilla and beat on medium-high speed until combined. Turn off the mixer and add about one-third of the flour mixture. Mix on low speed just until blended. Pour in about half of the coconut milk mixture and mix just until combined. Add about half of the remaining flour mixture and mix just until blended. Pour in the remaining coconut milk mixture and mix just until combined. Add the remaining flour mixture and mix just until blended. Turn off the mixer and scrape down the bowl. Using the spatula, stir in ½ cup of the crushed pineapple. (Reserve the remaining pineapple for another use.)

Fruit flowers

For a pretty garnish, cut a pineapple crosswise into thin slices, place the slices on a rack over a baking sheet, and bake in a 200°F oven until crisp.

COCONUT–CREAM CHEESE FROSTING

1 (8-ounce) package cream cheese, at room temperature

6 tablespoons (¾ stick) unsalted butter, at room temperature

1½ teaspoons coconut extract

1 teaspoon vanilla extract

2 cups powdered sugar

Dried pineapple flowers (see note) for garnish (optional)

Divide the batter evenly among the prepared muffin cups. Pour a little water into the empty muffin cups to prevent scorching. Bake until the tops are light golden brown and a wooden skewer inserted into the center of a cupcake comes out clean, 18 to 20 minutes. Using oven mitts, remove the pans from the oven and set them on a wire rack. Let the cupcakes cool in the pans for 10 minutes, then transfer them directly to the rack. Let cool completely, about 1 hour.

Meanwhile, prepare the frosting: In a large bowl, using an electric mixer, beat the cream cheese, butter, coconut, and vanilla on medium-high speed until light and fluffy, about 2 minutes. Turn off the mixer and scrape down the bowl with a rubber spatula. Add about half of the powdered sugar and mix on low speed until well blended. Turn off the mixer, add the remaining sugar, and beat on medium speed until smooth. The frosting should be spreadable; if it is too soft, cover the bowl and refrigerate it for about 15 minutes.

Fit a piping bag with a large plain tip. Place the bag tip-end down in a glass and carefully spoon the frosting into the piping bag using a rubber spatula, leaving about 2 inches free at the top. Gently twist the bag closed. Top the cupcakes with the frosting and decorate with the pineapple flowers (if using).

Neapolitan Ice Cream Cake

Classic ice cream flavors layered with chocolate cookie crumbles and covered in sweet whipped cream make for the perfect birthday cake, but you can use any ice cream flavor combo you like. It's best to start preparing this cake the day before you plan to serve it.

MAKES 8 TO 10 SERVINGS

1 pint each chocolate, strawberry, and vanilla ice cream, or your favorite flavors, homemade (page 87) or store-bought

7 ounces (about 20 cookies) store-bought chocolate sandwich cookies

1 cup heavy cream

2 tablespoons powdered sugar

Rainbow sprinkles for decorating

 Remove the chocolate ice cream from the freezer and let stand until soft enough to spread but not melted, about 10 minutes.

Meanwhile, place the cookies in a heavy-duty zippered plastic bag and seal shut. Using a rolling pin, roll over the cookies in the bag until crushed.

Transfer the softened chocolate ice cream to the bottom of a 9-inch springform pan and smooth with a small rubber spatula or icing spatula. Sprinkle half of the cookie crumbles on top and gently push them down with your fingers to form an even layer. Cover the pan with plastic wrap and place the pan on top of a plate lined with a paper towel (in case any melted ice cream leaks out). Freeze until the ice cream is no longer soft, 45 minutes to 1 hour.

About 10 minutes before the cake is frozen, remove the strawberry ice cream from the freezer to soften. Remove the pan from the freezer, transfer the softened strawberry ice cream to the pan, and smooth with the spatula. Sprinkle with the remaining cookie crumbles. Cover the pan with plastic wrap, place on the paper towel–lined plate, and freeze until the ice cream is no longer soft, 45 minutes to 1 hour.

About 10 minutes before the cake is frozen, remove the vanilla ice cream from the freezer to soften. Remove the pan from the freezer, transfer the softened vanilla ice cream to the pan, and smooth with the spatula. Cover the pan with plastic wrap, place on the paper towel–lined plate, and freeze until completely set, at least 4 hours or up to overnight.

~ Continued on page 46 ~

A slice of heaven

To make cutting the cake easier, dip a long, serrated cake knife into hot water, then wipe it dry before cutting a slice.

~ *Continued from page 45* ~

When the cake is completely frozen, carefully release the pan sides (you may need to run the clasp carefully under hot water for a few seconds to help it release). Return the cake to the paper towel–lined plate.

In a large bowl, using an electric mixer, beat the cream and powdered sugar on low speed until slightly thickened, 1 to 2 minutes. Gradually raise the speed to medium-high and beat until soft peaks form when the beaters are lifted (turn off the mixer first!), 2 to 3 minutes. Using an icing spatula or small rubber spatula and working quickly, spread the whipped cream over the top of the cake. Top with sprinkles.

Freeze the cake, uncovered, until set, about 1 hour. Cut the cake into slices and serve.

Chocolate Ice Box Cake

The longer this cake sits in the refrigerator, the tastier it gets. Allow at least a few hours for it to set, or make it a few days ahead of when you want to serve it. Leftover cookies can be crumbled and used to decorate the top of the cake.

MAKES 10 TO 12 SERVINGS

CHOCOLATE COOKIES

1¼ cups all-purpose flour, plus flour for dusting

¾ cup granulated sugar

¾ cup unsweetened cocoa powder

1 teaspoon baking soda

½ teaspoon salt

¼ teaspoon baking powder

12 tablespoons (1½ sticks) unsalted butter, at room temperature

1 large egg plus 1 large egg yolk

WHIPPED CREAM

3 cups heavy cream

2 teaspoons vanilla extract

½ cup powdered sugar

 Preheat the oven to 375°F. Line 2 cookie sheets with parchment paper.

To make the cookies, in a large bowl, whisk together the flour, granulated sugar, cocoa powder, baking soda, salt, and baking powder. Add the butter and, using an electric mixer, beat on low speed for 2 minutes. Add the egg and egg yolk and beat on low speed until a dough forms, about 1 minute. Turn off the mixer and scrape down the bowl with a rubber spatula.

Dump the dough onto a lightly floured work surface. Using a floured rolling pin, roll out the dough until it is about ¼ inch thick. Using a 2 ½-inch round cookie cutter, cut out as many cookies as possible. Transfer the cookies to the prepared cookie sheets, spacing them about 1 inch apart. Press the dough scraps together, roll out, and cut out more cookies. If the dough is too sticky to roll, wrap it in plastic wrap and refrigerate until slightly firm, about 15 minutes.

When both cookie sheets are full, bake 1 cookie sheet at a time until the centers of the cookies are firm to the touch, 8 to 10 minutes. Using oven mitts, remove the cookie sheet from the oven and set it on a wire rack. Let cool for 5 minutes, then use a metal spatula to move the cookies directly to the rack. Repeat to bake the rest of the cookies. Let cool completely.

Time-saving tip

Need dessert in a hurry? Skip the homemade cookies here and sub in two dozen purchased chocolate wafer cookies instead.

To make the whipped cream, in a large bowl, using an electric mixer, beat the cream, vanilla, and powdered sugar on medium speed until soft peaks form when the beaters are lifted (turn off the mixer first!), 2 to 3 minutes.

To assemble, place the cookies in a single layer, as close together as possible, in a 9-by-3-inch round cake pan or ceramic dish. If needed, break some cookies in half to fill in the center of the circle. Spread a thick layer of the whipped cream on top of the cookies. Top with another layer of cookies, followed by another layer of whipped cream. Repeat until you reach the top of the pan, ending with a layer of whipped cream. Crumble any remaining cookies and sprinkle them on top of the cake, if desired. Cover the pan with plastic wrap and refrigerate until set, at least 4 hours or up to 3 days. Cut the cake into slices and serve cold.

Lemon Meringue Cookies

The pretty yellow swirls of these lemony treats might look fancy but are really quite easy to create. Simply paint the inside of a piping bag with vertical stripes of yellow food coloring before adding the meringue mixture.

MAKES ABOUT 24 COOKIES

Nonstick cooking spray

4 large egg whites, at room temperature

1 teaspoon salt

2 cups powdered sugar, sifted

1 teaspoon lemon extract

Yellow food coloring

Line 2 cookie sheets with parchment paper. Using a 2-inch circular guide (such as a biscuit cutter), draw 12 circles on each parchment sheet. Remove the parchment from the cookie sheets and lightly spray the cookie sheets with nonstick cooking spray. Turn the parchment over and place on the cookie sheets; you should be able to see the circles through the paper.

In a large bowl, using an electric mixer, beat the egg whites on medium-high speed until foamy, about 1 minute. Add the salt and continue beating on medium-high speed until a dense foam forms, about 1 minute. Beating continuously, gradually add the powdered sugar about 2 tablespoons at a time, then continue to beat until the mixture is glossy and very fluffy, about 5 minutes. Add the lemon extract and beat just until combined, about 1 minute.

Fit a large piping bag with a ½-inch star tip. Using a small, clean paintbrush, paint 4 long vertical stripes of food coloring up the inside of the bag, spacing them equally between the top, bottom, left, and right sides of the bag.

Place the bag tip-end down in a glass and carefully spoon the batter into the piping bag using a rubber spatula, trying not to disturb the lines of food coloring; leave about 2 inches free at the top. Gently twist the bag closed.

~ *Continued on page 52* ~

Storage tip

To keep meringues crispy, make sure they are dry before taking them out of the oven and store them in an airtight container.

〜 *Continued from page 51* 〜

Pipe the batter onto the prepared cookie sheets, starting at the edge of each traced circle, moving the bag in a circular motion, and working your way around to the center of the traced circle so that the batter forms a coil. Refill the piping bag with any remaining batter (add more food coloring stripes before adding the remaining batter if needed) and pipe more circles. Let stand at room temperature, uncovered, for 30 minutes.

Meanwhile, preheat the oven to 250°F.

Bake 1 cookie sheet at a time until the cookies are firm and dry to the touch, 25 to 30 minutes, rotating the cookie sheet about halfway through baking (ask an adult for help). If they still feel tacky, turn off the oven and let them remain in the oven until completely dry. Using oven mitts, remove the cookie sheet from the oven and set it on a wire rack. Repeat to bake the rest of the cookies. Let the cookies cool completely on the cookie sheets and serve.

Apricot Streusel Coffeecake

This fruity, streusel-topped cake is the perfect way to kick off a summer day. Apricots are a yummy addition, but you can substitute them with other seasonal fruits, if you like. Diced fresh peaches, sliced plums, or blackberries would also be delicious.

MAKES 12 SERVINGS

2 cups all-purpose flour, plus 1 tablespoon

½ teaspoon baking powder

½ teaspoon baking soda

½ teaspoon salt

1 cup unsalted butter

1¾ cups granulated sugar

2 large eggs

1 teaspoon vanilla extract

1 cup sour cream

8 ripe apricots, pitted and diced

2 tablespoons firmly packed light brown sugar

1 teaspoon ground cinnamon

PECAN STREUSEL

¾ cup all-purpose flour

⅓ cup firmly packed light brown sugar

6 tablespoons unsalted butter, at room temperature

1 cup chopped pecans

 Preheat the oven to 350°F (180°C). Lightly butter a 9-by-13-inch baking dish. Dust the dish with flour, tapping out the excess.

In a bowl, sift together the 2 cups flour, baking powder, baking soda, and salt. In another bowl, using an electric mixer, beat the butter and granulated sugar on high speed until light and fluffy, about 3 minutes. Beat in the eggs one at a time, beating well after each addition. Beat in the vanilla. Reduce the speed to low and add the dry ingredients in three additions alternately with the sour cream in two additions, beginning and ending with the dry ingredients and beating until smooth after each addition.

In a small bowl, gently stir together the apricots, brown sugar, cinnamon, and the 1 tablespoon flour. Spread half of the batter in the prepared dish. Top with the apricot mixture. Spread the remaining batter over the apricot mixture, smoothing the top.

To make the streusel, in a small bowl, stir together the flour, brown sugar, and butter. Using your fingers, work the ingredients together just until combined. Mix in the pecans. Press into a ball, and then separate with your fingers into coarse crumbs. Sprinkle the streusel evenly over the batter.

Bake until a toothpick inserted into the center of the cake comes out clean, about 45 minutes. Using oven mitts, remove the pan from the oven and set it on a wire rack. Let cool for 15 minutes. Cut the cake into squares and serve.

Fruity fun
If you can't find a watermelon big enough to yield three thick layers, try using two watermelons instead.

Fruity Cake Tower

Three layers of dense, seedless watermelon and a creative spray of fresh seasonal fruit are all that's required for this impressive summertime treat. Use skewers to secure the layers in place and to attach the pieces of fruit; just be sure to remove them before slicing.

MAKES 10 TO 12 SERVINGS

1 large oblong
seedless watermelon

1 cup mixed berries,
such as strawberries,
blackberries, and
blueberries

Fresh mint leaves
for garnish

Ask an adult to help you cut the watermelon: Using a large knife, cut off the ends of the watermelon and discard, then cut it crosswise into 3 pieces of equal thickness. Place the largest piece, cut side down, on a cutting board; set the other pieces aside. Find a plate or a bowl that is slightly smaller than the circumference of the watermelon. Turn the plate upside down on the large piece of watermelon and trace along its edge with the tip of a knife to make a perfect circle. Remove the plate and using a sharp knife (ask an adult for help), cut along the traced edge to remove the rind and form a cylinder shape. Place the cylinder, cut side down, on a rimmed cake plate to make the bottom "cake" layer and insert 3 wooden skewers or chopsticks into the center, leaving 2 inches of each skewer exposed.

Repeat the cutting process with the other two watermelon pieces, using two more plates, each one about 2 inches smaller in width than the one used before it. Place the middle watermelon layer over the bottom layer, centering it and pressing it onto the skewers. Insert 2 wooden skewers or chopsticks into the center of the middle layer, leaving 2 inches of each skewer exposed. Place the smallest watermelon layer on top, centering it and pressing it gently onto the skewers. Save any remaining watermelon for another use.

Arrange the berries on top and around each layer, using more skewers to secure each berry to the cake, if necessary. Garnish with mint leaves.

To serve, remove the berries and set aside. Remove the skewers and discard. Cut the watermelon cake into pieces, top with the berries, and serve.

Seven Layer Bars

You won't need a mixing bowl and spoon to make these yummy bars. Just layer the ingredients in the dish and bake. If you like, trade half of the bittersweet chocolate chips for white chocolate chips, or substitute peanut butter chips for the butterscotch chips.

MAKES 20 BARS

About 10 graham crackers

½ cup (1 stick) unsalted butter, cut into pieces

1½ cups bittersweet chocolate chips

1 cup butterscotch chips

1 cup old-fashioned oats

1 cup pecans, toasted and chopped

1 cup walnuts, toasted and chopped

1 (14-oz) can sweetened condensed milk

1½ cups shredded dried unsweetened coconut

Preheat the oven to 350°F.

Place the graham crackers in a heavy-duty zippered plastic bag and seal shut. Using a rolling pin, roll over the crackers in the bag until finely ground. You should have about 1½ cups crumbs.

Put the butter in a 9-by-13-inch baking dish and transfer to the oven. When the butter has melted, remove the baking dish from the oven and carefully swirl the dish to coat the bottom and sides. Spread the graham cracker crumbs in an even layer over the bottom of the dish. Layer the chocolate chips, butterscotch chips, oats, pecans, and walnuts on top. Pour the condensed milk over the entire surface. Sprinkle the coconut on top.

Bake until the coconut is toasted and the edges are golden brown, 20 to 25 minutes. Using oven mitts, remove the baking dish from the oven and set it on a wire rack. Let cool completely. Cut into 20 bars and serve.

S'mores Brownies

When you want an ooey, gooey, chocolaty s'more but don't have a campfire handy, these s'mores brownies are just the thing. Keep a close eye on the marshmallows—they can burn just as easily in the oven as they do over a fire.

MAKES 12 BROWNIES

1 cup all-purpose flour

½ teaspoon baking soda

½ teaspoon salt

12 tablespoons
(1½ sticks) unsalted
butter, plus butter
for greasing

6 ounces unsweetened
chocolate, finely chopped

1 cup granulated sugar

1 cup firmly packed
light brown sugar

4 large eggs, at room
temperature

¼ cup light corn syrup,
honey, or maple syrup

2 teaspoons
vanilla extract

6 graham crackers

12 jumbo marshmallows

Preheat the oven to 350°F. Butter a 9-by-13-inch baking pan.

In a medium bowl, sift together the flour, baking soda, and salt. Set aside. Put the butter in a saucepan. Set the pan over medium heat and melt the butter. Remove from the heat and add the chocolate. Let stand for 3 minutes, then whisk until smooth. Whisk in both sugars until blended. Add the eggs 1 at a time, whisking well after each addition. Add the corn syrup and vanilla and whisk until blended. Add the flour mixture and stir until combined.

Scrape the batter into the prepared pan, spreading it evenly. Crush the graham crackers with your hands and scatter them evenly over the top.

Bake for 20 minutes. Using oven mitts, remove the pan from the oven, then carefully drop the marshmallows over the graham crackers, spacing them evenly. Continue to bake until a wooden skewer inserted into the center comes out with a few moist crumbs attached, 5 to 7 minutes. Use the oven mitts to remove the pan from the oven and set it on a wire rack. Let cool, then cut into 12 squares and serve.

Pies, Tarts & Crumbles

★

Classic Peach Pie

Partially baking the bottom crust before filling it with peaches may seem like a hassle, but the little bit of extra effort is worth it. You'll be rewarded with a bottom crust that is every bit as flaky and light as the top one.

MAKES 8 TO 10 SERVINGS

PIE PASTRY

3 cups all-purpose flour

2 teaspoons sugar

1 teaspoon salt

1 cup very cold unsalted butter, cut into cubes

½ cup ice-cold water, or more if needed

PEACH FILLING

2 pounds peaches

1 tablespoon lemon juice

⅓ cup sugar, plus sugar for sprinkling

¼ teaspoon salt

¼ teaspoon ground cinnamon

¼ cup all-purpose flour, plus flour for dusting

2 tablespoons unsalted butter, cut into pieces

1 large egg white, beaten with 1 teaspoon water

To make the pie pastry, in a bowl, mix the flour, sugar, and salt. Scatter the butter over the flour mixture. Using a pastry blender or two knives, cut in the butter until the mixture resembles coarse crumbs. Sprinkle the water over the top and, using a fork, mix lightly until the dough begins to hold together in large clumps. If the dough is too crumbly, mix in a little more water, 1 teaspoon at a time. Dump the dough onto a work surface and press into a mound. Divide the dough in half. Wrap each half in plastic wrap, then press each half into a disk. Refrigerate for at least 1 hour or up to 3 days.

To make the peach filling, fill a large saucepan three-fourths full of water. Set the pan over high heat and bring the water to a boil. Gently lower the peaches into the boiling water with a slotted spoon. Let boil for 30 seconds, then remove them with the slotted spoon and transfer them to a clean work surface. When cool enough to handle, slip off the skins, using your fingertips or a paring knife. Using a paring knife, make a cut all the way around the peach, from stem end to blossom end and back. Gently twist the fruit to separate the two halves and remove the pit. Cut each peach half into ½-inch slices and transfer to a bowl. Add the lemon juice and toss to coat the peaches evenly. Stir in the sugar, salt, and cinnamon.

Preheat the oven to 375°F.

~ Continued on page 62 ~

~ *Continued from page 61* ~

Remove 1 dough disk from the refrigerator and let stand at room temperature for 5 minutes. Sprinkle a work surface with flour. Remove the dough disk from the plastic wrap and place it on the floured surface. Using a rolling pin, roll out the dough into a round at least 12 inches in diameter and about ⅛ inch thick. Fold the dough round in half, then into quarters, and transfer it to a 9-inch pie pan, positioning the point at the center. Unfold the dough, press it into the pan, and trim the edges flush with the pan rim. Place in the freezer for 15 minutes.

Prick the pastry in the pie dish all over with a fork. Bake just until golden, about 15 minutes. Using oven mitts, remove the pie dish from the oven and set it on a wire rack. Let cool slightly.

Sprinkle the flour over the peaches and toss to distribute evenly. Set aside.

Remove the remaining dough disk from the refrigerator and let stand at room temperature for 5 minutes. Sprinkle a work surface with flour. Remove the plastic wrap and place the dough on the floured surface. Using a rolling pin, roll out the dough into a 10-inch round. Pour the peaches into the partially baked pie shell and dot with the butter. Transfer the pastry round to the pie, positioning it over the filling. Trim the dough edges flush with the pan rim. Lift the edge of the top pastry round and, using a pastry brush, brush the rim of bottom pie pastry with the egg white mixture. Gently press the top pastry onto the bottom pastry. Using your thumb and forefinger, pinch the dough decoratively along the pie rim, sealing the edge of the top and bottom crusts in the process. Cut 5 or 6 slits in the top pastry to vent the steam. Brush the top lightly with the egg white mixture, then sprinkle with sugar.

Bake the pie until the crust is golden and the filling is thick and bubbling, 50 to 60 minutes. Using oven mitts, remove the pie dish from the oven and set it on a wire rack. Let cool completely. Cut the pie into wedges and serve.

Pack a picnic
Cookies and hand pies are classic picnic fare, but even ice pops and whole fruit pies can be made easily portable.

Apple Galettes

These rustic pastries are like flat, open-faced fruit pies. For a sweet and crusty finish, brush the pastry edges with egg white and sprinkle with sugar before baking. Serve each galette with a small scoop of your favorite ice cream on top.

MAKES 6 SMALL GALETTES

Pie Pastry (page 61)

4 apples, preferably Granny Smith or Pippin, peeled, cored, and sliced ¼ inch thick

Finely grated zest of 1 lemon

1 tablespoon lemon juice

¼ cup sugar

½ teaspoon ground cinnamon

Pinch of salt

All-purpose flour for dusting

Vanilla or dulce de leche ice cream for serving

 Prepare the pie dough, shape into a large, flat disk, and chill as directed. Line 2 baking sheets with parchment paper.

In a large bowl, toss together the apples, lemon zest, lemon juice, sugar, the cinnamon, and salt. Set aside.

Remove the dough disk from the refrigerator and let stand at room temperature for 5 minutes. Sprinkle a work surface with flour. Remove the dough disk from the plastic wrap and place it on the floured surface. Cut the dough into 6 equal pieces. Using a rolling pin, roll each piece into a round about ⅛ inch thick. Transfer the dough rounds to the prepared baking sheets, spacing them evenly. Divide the apple mixture evenly among the rounds, spreading it in an even layer and leaving a 1-inch border of dough uncovered along the edge. Fold the edge of the dough up and over the apples, loosely pleating the dough and leaving the galettes uncovered in the center. Refrigerate the galettes for about 30 minutes.

Meanwhile, preheat the oven to 400°F.

Bake the galettes until the crust is golden brown and the apples are tender, about 40 minutes. Using oven mitts, remove the baking sheets from the oven and set them on a wire rack. Let cool briefly. Serve each galette warm or at room temperature with a small scoop of ice cream on top.

Key Lime Pie with Pretzel Crust

Key limes grow in the Florida Keys during the summer months, though those grown in Mexico and Central America are available year-round. If you can't find Key limes, look for bottled Key lime juice and substitute the zest with 2 teaspoons regular lime zest.

MAKES 8 TO 10 SERVINGS

PRETZEL CRUST

4½ cups (about 6 ounces) pretzels

1 tablespoon firmly packed light brown sugar

½ cup unsatled butter, melted and cooled

Pinch of salt

FILLING

8 large egg yolks

2 (14-fluid-ounce) cans sweetened condensed milk

4 teaspoons finely grated Key lime zest, plus lime zest for garnish (optional)

1 cup Key lime juice

Turbinado sugar for sprinkling (optional)

To make the crust, preheat the oven to 350°F. In the bowl of a food processor, pulse the pretzels until finely ground. Add the brown sugar, melted butter, and salt and pulse until the mixture resembles wet sand. Pour the pretzel mixture into a 9½-inch pie pan and press gently with your fingers to spread it evenly across the bottom and up the sides of the pan.

Bake until the crust is golden brown, about 10 minutes. Transfer to a wire rack and let cool completely. Leave the oven set at 350°F.

To make the filling, in a large bowl, whisk together the egg yolks until well blended. Add the condensed milk and lime zest and juice and whisk until combined. Pour the filling into the cooled crust. Place the pie dish on a baking sheet.

Bake until the edges of the pie are set but the center still jiggles slightly (ask an adult for help), 18 to 22 minutes. Using oven mitts, remove the pie dish from the oven and set it on a wire rack. Let cool completely. Garnish the pie with lime zest and sprinkle with turbinado sugar, if you like. Cover the pie with plastic wrap and refrigerate for at least 2 hours or up to overnight before serving. Cut the pie into wedges and serve.

Lemon-Confetti Whoopie Pies

At your next birthday party, skip the traditional cake and opt for these colorful, flavorful treats, which have the icing inside the cake instead. Prepare a few batches of filling in different colors for a mix of vibrant hues.

MAKES 15 WHOOPIE PIES OR 30 MINI WHOOPIE PIES

CAKES

2 cups all-purpose flour

1½ teaspoons baking soda

½ teaspoon salt

6 tablespoons (¾ stick) unsalted butter, at room temperature

½ cup firmly packed light brown sugar

½ cup granulated sugar

1 tablespoon finely grated lemon zest

1 large egg

1 cup buttermilk

1 teaspoon vanilla extract

2 tablespoons nonpareil sprinkles

Position 2 racks in the oven so that they are evenly spaced and preheat the oven to 350°F. Line 2 cookie sheets with parchment paper.

To make the cakes, in a medium bowl, whisk together the flour, baking soda, and salt. In a large bowl, using an electric mixer, beat the butter and both sugars on medium speed until light and fluffy, 2 to 3 minutes. Turn off the mixer and scrape down the bowl with a rubber spatula. Add the lemon zest and beat on medium speed until combined. Add the egg and beat until blended. Turn off the mixer and add about half of the flour mixture. Mix on low speed just until blended. Pour in the buttermilk and vanilla and mix just until combined. Add the remaining flour mixture and mix just until blended. Turn off the mixer and scrape down the bowl. Using a rubber spatula, gently fold in the sprinkles.

Spray a a small ice cream scoop (for standard whoopie pies) or a teaspoon (for mini pies) with cooking spray. Drop scoops of the batter onto the prepared cookie sheets, spacing them about 2 inches apart.

Bake both cookie sheets at the same time until the tops of the cakes are golden and firm to the touch, 9 to 10 minutes for the standard pies or 8 minutes for the mini pies. Using oven mitts, remove the cookie sheets from the oven and set them on wire racks. Let cool for 5 minutes, then use a metal spatula to move the cakes directly to the racks. Let cool completely, about 30 minutes.

~ Continued on page 68 ~

~ *Continued from page 67* ~

FILLING

½ cup (1 stick) unsalted
butter, at room
temperature

2½ cups powdered sugar

3 tablespoons whole milk

½ teaspoon vanilla extract

½ teaspoon lemon extract

Pinch of salt

Selection of food colorings,
such as pink, blue, purple,
and/or yellow

Meanwhile, make the filling: In a large bowl, using an electric mixer, beat the butter on medium speed until light and fluffy, about 2 minutes. Turn off the mixer and scrape down the bowl with a rubber spatula. Add the powdered sugar, milk, vanilla and lemon extracts, and salt and mix on low speed just until combined. Turn off the mixer and scrape down the bowl. Beat on medium-high speed until the filling is airy and smooth, about 5 minutes.

If making multiple colors of filling, divide the filling into smaller bowls, add a few drops of food coloring to each bowl (1 color per bowl), and stir to combine. Add more food coloring if needed until the desired color is reached.

Fit a piping bag with a round tip or snip the corner from a plastic bag. (If using multiple colors, you will need a separate piping bag for each color.) Place the bag tip-end down in a glass and carefully spoon the filling into the piping bag using a rubber spatula, leaving about 2 inches free at the top. Gently twist the bag closed. Pipe the filling onto the flat side of one cake and top with another cake, flat side down, to create a sandwich. Repeat to fill and assemble the remaining cakes.

Piping perfection
For the best results when piping frosting, squeeze the piping bag from the top to force the frosting towards the tip.

Individual Cherry Cobblers

A cobbler consists of a biscuitlike topping and a fresh fruit filling. The soft biscuit dough spreads as it bakes to cover the cherries completely, like an upside-down pie. Serve with a dollop of whipped cream or a scoop of vanilla ice cream, if you like.

MAKES 6 COBBLERS

FILLING

3 pounds fresh Bing cherries or other sweet cherries, pitted

1 tablespoon lemon juice

3 tablespoons sugar

TOPPING

⅔ cup buttermilk

1 teaspoon vanilla extract

1½ cups all-purpose flour

⅓ cup plus 1 tablespoon sugar

1 teaspoon baking powder

½ teaspoon baking soda

½ teaspoon salt

¾ teaspoon ground cinnamon

6 tablespoons (¾ stick) cold unsalted butter, cut into ½-inch pieces

Preheat the oven to 375°F. Place six 1-cup ramekins or custard cups on a baking sheet.

To make the filling, in a large bowl, toss together the cherries, lemon juice, and sugar. Divide the mixture evenly among the ramekins. Bake for 10 minutes.

Meanwhile, make the topping: In a small bowl, stir together the buttermilk and vanilla; set aside. In a large bowl, sift together the flour, the ⅓ cup sugar, the baking powder, baking soda, salt, and ½ teaspoon of the cinnamon. Add the butter and, using a pastry blender or 2 knives, cut the butter into the flour mixture until large, coarse crumbs the size of small peas form. Pour the buttermilk mixture over the flour mixture and, using a wooden spoon, stir just until combined and a soft, sticky, evenly moistened dough forms.

Using oven mitts, remove the baking sheet from the oven. Drop the dough by heaping spoonfuls onto the hot fruit, spacing it evenly over the surface. The topping will not completely cover the fruit but will spread during baking. In a small bowl, stir together the remaining 1 tablespoon sugar and ¼ teaspoon cinnamon. Sprinkle over the dough.

Bake until the fruit filling is bubbling, the topping is browned, and a wooden skewer inserted into the topping comes out clean, 30 to 35 minutes. Using the oven mitts, remove the baking sheet from the oven and set it on a wire rack. Let cool for 15 minutes. Serve warm.

Jumbo July 4th Whoopie Pies

Extra-large red velvet cake sandwiches are super fun, but you can make these festive treats in any size you like—just use a smaller ice cream scoop. The cream cheese filling is addictive (and also equally delicious atop your favorite cupcakes).

MAKES 10 LARGE WHOOPIE PIES

CAKES

4 cups all-purpose flour

¼ cup unsweetened cocoa powder

2 teaspoons salt

2 teaspoons baking soda

½ teaspoon baking powder

1 cup buttermilk

2 tablespoons red food coloring, plus more as needed

2 teaspoons vanilla extract

1 cup (2 sticks) unsalted butter, at room temperature

1¾ cups granulated sugar

2 large eggs

Nonstick cooking spray

Position 2 racks in the oven so that they are evenly spaced and preheat the oven to 350°F. Line 2 cookie sheets with parchment paper.

To make the cakes, in a large bowl, whisk together the flour, cocoa powder, salt, baking soda, and baking powder. Pour the buttermilk into a measuring cup, add the red food coloring and vanilla, and whisk to combine. The milk should be deep red, so add more food coloring if needed.

In a large bowl, using an electric mixer, beat the butter and granulated sugar on medium-high speed until light and fluffy, about 4 minutes. Turn off the mixer and scrape down the bowl with a rubber spatula. Add the eggs one at a time, beating well after each addition. Turn off the mixer and add about one-third of the flour mixture. Mix on low speed just until blended. Pour in about half of the buttermilk mixture and mix just until combined. Add about half of the remaining flour mixture and mix just until blended. Pour in the remaining buttermilk mixture and mix just until combined. Add the remaining flour mixture and mix until completely blended. Turn off the mixer and scrape down the bowl. The batter should be deep red; add more food coloring if needed and mix until combined.

Spray an ice cream scoop with nonstick cooking spray and drop 20 scoops of the batter onto the prepared cookie sheets, spacing them about 3 inches apart. (If the batter starts to stick, spray the ice cream scoop occasionally in between scoops.)

Festive swirls

Layer blue and white frosting in the same piping bag to create a fun, two-tone filling for whoopie pies.

Bake both cookie sheets at the same time until the cakes are firm to the touch and spring back when lightly touched, 13 to 15 minutes. Remove the cookie sheets from the oven and set them on wire racks. Let cool for 10 minutes, then use a metal spatula to move the cakes directly to the racks. Let cool completely, about 30 minutes.

FILLING

12 tablespoons (1½ sticks) unsalted butter, at room temperature

2 (8-ounce) packages cream cheese, at room temperature

4 cups powdered sugar

Blue food coloring

Meanwhile, make the filling: In a large bowl, using an electric mixer, beat the butter and cream cheese on medium-high speed until combined, about 2 minutes. Turn off the mixer and scrape down the bowl with a rubber spatula. Add the powdered sugar and beat on medium-high speed until fluffy, about 5 minutes.

Fit a piping bag with a star tip. Place the bag tip-end down in a glass and carefully spoon half of the filling to one side of the piping bag, leaving about 2 inches free at the top. Add a few drops of blue food coloring to the remaining filling and stir to combine. Add more food coloring if needed until the desired color is reached. Carefully spoon the blue filling into the other side of the piping bag (it's OK if the fillings mix a little, but you should have two distinct sides of filling). Gently twist the bag closed. Pipe the filling onto the flat side of one cake and top with another cake, flat side down, to create a sandwich. Repeat to fill and assemble the remaining cakes.

Lemon Curd & Kiwi Tartlets

Kiwi gives a unexpected flourish to these lemon curd–filled tartlets, though feel free to substitute summer berries instead. To prevent the tartlet shells from shrinking during baking, make sure each pastry-lined pan is well chilled before putting it in the oven.

MAKES 24 TWO-INCH TARTLETS

LEMON CURD

1 whole egg

4 egg yolks

½ cup sugar

⅓ cup fresh lemon juice

2 tablespoons unsalted butter, cubed

Pie Pastry (page 61) or purchased pie pastry for double-crust 9-inch pie

6 kiwi fruits

To make the lemon curd, in a heatproof bowl set over (not touching) barely simmering water in a saucepan, whisk together the whole egg, egg yolks, sugar, and lemon juice. Cook, stirring constantly, until thickened, 5 to 8 minutes. To test if it is ready, pull the spoon out of the bowl and draw your finger across the back of it; if your finger leaves a trail that does not fill in immediately, the curd is ready.

Remove from the heat and add the butter, stirring until incorporated. Strain through a fine-mesh sieve into another bowl. Cover with plastic wrap, pressing it directly onto the surface of the curd (this helps prevent a skin from forming). Refrigerate until well chilled and set, about 3 hours.

Make the pie pastry and refrigerate as directed.

Have ready 24 2-inch tartlet pans or a 24-well mini muffin pan. On a lightly floured work surface, roll out the dough about ¼ inch thick. Using a round pastry cutter about 2-inches in diameter, cut out as many rounds as possible. One at a time, transfer the dough rounds to the tartlet pans, gently pressing the dough onto the bottom and up the sides of each pan and trimming off

~ Continued on page 76 ~

Perfect shells

Prick the dough lining the tart shells with the tines of a fork to help prevent the pastry from buckling in the oven.

~ *Continued from page 75* ~

any overhang. Gather up the dough scraps, press together, reroll, cut out more rounds, and line the remaining pans. Place the lined pans on a sheet pan and place in the freezer until well chilled, about 30 minutes. About 15 minutes before the tartlet shells are ready to bake, preheat the oven to 375°F.

Using a fork, prick the bottom and sides of the pastry lining each shell. Bake the tartlet shells until golden, 12–14 minutes. Transfer to a wire rack and let cool completely.

While the tart shells are cooling, using a small knife, cut the peel from the kiwi fruits. Cut the fruits lengthwise, then cut crosswise into slices. Set aside.

Carefully remove the cooled tartlet shells from the pans. Fill the shells with the lemon curd, dividing it evenly and spreading it in an even layer. Top each tartlet with a slice of kiwi fruit and serve.

Raspberry & Apricot Crumble

This sweet and juicy crumble features two of the season's most delicate fruits.
You can bake the apricots and raspberries in one big dish, or divide them between
individual ramekins, scattering the sweet crumble topping over the fruit.

MAKES 8 SERVINGS

TOPPING

1½ cups all-purpose flour

¾ cup sugar

1 teaspoon salt

1 cup (2 sticks) cold
unsalted butter,
cut into cubes

1 cup old-fashioned oats

FILLING

3 pounds apricots,
halved, pitted, and sliced

4 cups raspberries

½ cup sugar

¼ cup all-purpose flour

To make the topping, in the bowl of a food processor, combine the flour, sugar, and salt. Pulse until combined. Add the butter and pulse until the mixture resembles coarse crumbs. Add the oats and pulse to combine. Transfer to a medium bowl.

To make the filling, in a large bowl, toss together the apricots, raspberries, sugar, and flour. Spread the fruit mixture in a 9-by-13-inch baking dish. Using your fingers, press the topping into large clumps and scatter evenly over the fruit. Alternatively, divide the fruit and topping evenly among eight ½-cup ramekins.

Bake until the topping is golden and crisp and the fruit is bubbling, about 1 hour for the baking dish and about 30 minutes for the ramekins. Remove the baking dish or ramekins from the oven and set on a wire rack. Let cool for at least 10 minutes. Serve warm or at room temperature. If using a baking dish, scoop up portions of the crumble into bowls.

Blackberry Tart with Pecan Crust

When fresh berries are in season, they need very little sugar to enhance their natural sweetness. You can use blueberries in place of the blackberries, if you like. For a nut-free crust, omit the pecans and use 1¼ cups all-purpose flour instead.

MAKES 8 SERVINGS

CRUST

1 cup pecan halves

¾ cup all-purpose flour

3 tablespoons sugar

½ teaspoon salt

½ cup (1 stick) unsalted butter, at room temperature

1 tablespoon white vinegar

FILLING

⅓ to ½ cup sugar

2 tablespoons all-purpose flour

Dash of ground cinnamon

4 cups blackberries

Whipped cream or ice cream for serving (optional)

Preheat the oven to 375°F. Trace the bottom of a 9-inch tart pan with a removable bottom onto a sheet of parchment paper and cut out the circle with scissors. Put the paper circle in the bottom of the pan.

To make the crust, in the bowl of a food processor, grind the pecans until fine crumbs form. Transfer to a bowl. Add the flour, sugar, and salt, and stir until combined. Add the butter and, using a pastry blender or two knives, cut the butter into the nut mixture until large crumbs form. Add the vinegar and mix gently with the fork until the dough comes together.

Pour the nut mixture into the prepared tart pan and press gently with your fingers to spread it evenly across the bottom and up the sides of the pan.

To make the filling, in a large bowl, whisk together the sugar, flour, and cinnamon. Add the blackberries and stir gently to mix. Pour the berry mixture over the crust, spreading evenly. Place the pan on a cookie sheet.

Bake the tart for 40 minutes. Cover the tart loosely with aluminum foil to prevent burning (ask an adult for help if needed!), then continue to bake until the berries are bursting and the crust is deep brown, 20 to 25 minutes longer.

Using oven mitts, remove the cookie sheet from the oven and set the tart pan on a wire rack. Let cool. Remove the outer rim of the pan and place the tart on a serving plate. Cut into slices. Serve with whipped cream or ice cream, if you like.

Strawberry Hand Pies

Whether you're enjoying a picnic at the park, a day at the beach, or a poolside snack, these hand pies are the perfect portable dessert. An egg wash brushed over the pies before baking creates a shiny, golden-brown sheen in the oven.

MAKES 4 HAND PIES

1 cup strawberries, sliced

2 tablespoons water

¼ cup sugar, plus sugar for sprinkling

2 tablespoons cornstarch

Pinch of salt

All-purpose flour for dusting

1 sheet frozen puff pastry, thawed

1 egg

1 tablespoon milk

In a saucepan, combine the strawberries, water, sugar, cornstarch, and salt. Set the pan over low heat and cook, stirring constantly, until the mixture is thick and jamlike, about 5 minutes. Transfer the strawberries to a bowl and cover with plastic wrap, pressing it directly onto the surface of the berries. Refrigerate until completely cool, about 1 hour.

Line a baking sheet with parchment paper. Sprinkle a work surface with flour. Place the puff pastry on the floured surface. Roll out and/or cut the pastry as needed to make an even 10-inch square. Cut the pastry into 4 equal squares. Divide the strawberry filling evenly among the squares, placing it in the center of each one. Lightly brush the edges of each square with water and fold into a triangle. Gently press the edges together with the tines of a fork to seal. Place the turnovers on the prepared baking sheet, spacing them about 2 inches apart, and refrigerate for 15 minutes.

Meanwhile, preheat the oven to 375°F.

In a cup, whisk together the egg and milk. Using a pastry brush, brush the egg wash over the tops of the pies, then sprinkle with sugar. Bake until puffed and golden brown, 25 to 35 minutes. Using oven mitts, remove the baking sheet from the oven and set it on a wire rack. Let cool for 20 minutes, then serve warm.

Nectarine-Blueberry Crisp

Sweet-tart nectarines and juicy blueberries are covered with a crunchy layer of spiced oats in this classic dessert. To get a head start, prepare the fruit filling and the crisp topping and refrigerate for up to 1 day, then assemble and bake right before serving.

MAKES 8 TO 10 SERVINGS

½ cup rolled oats

½ cup firmly packed light brown sugar

¼ cup all-purpose flour

¼ cup finely chopped almonds or pecans

½ teaspoon ground cinnamon

¼ teaspoon ground nutmeg

¼ teaspoon salt

6 tablespoons butter, at room temperature

4 nectarines or peaches (about 2 lb/1 kg), peeled (see page 61 for the technique) and sliced

1 cup (about 4 oz/120 g) blackberries

Vanilla ice cream for serving (optional)

 Preheat the oven to 375°F. In a small bowl, stir together the oats, brown sugar, flour, nuts, cinnamon, nutmeg, and salt. Using your fingertips, rub the butter into the oat mixture until well blended and crumbly.

In eight 8-oz gratin dishes or one 9 x 13-inch baking dish, combine the peaches and blackberries and spread in an even layer. Scatter the topping evenly over the fruit.

Bake until the juices are bubbling and the topping is richly browned, 30 to 35 minutes. Using oven mitts, remove the crisp from the oven and let cool slightly. Scoop individual portions of the crisp onto serving plates or serve in the individual gratin dishes. Serve warm or at room temperature, accompanied by vanilla ice cream, if desired.

Cool Sweets

★

Mud Pie Sundae

Layers of coffee ice cream, chocolate cookie crumbles, and sweet whipped cream are the classic mud pie trio. Pack these individually sized mud pies in jars for portable treats. Set out any leftover toppings and invite your friends to load up their jars even more!

MAKES 4 SERVINGS

FUDGE SAUCE

½ cup heavy cream

½ cup (1 stick) unsalted butter, cut into pieces

½ cup light corn syrup

½ cup powdered sugar

9 ounces bittersweet chocolate, chopped

1 teaspoon vanilla extract

WHIPPED CREAM

1 cup heavy cream

1 tablespoon granulated sugar

1 teaspoon vanilla extract

4 ounces chocolate wafer cookies

1 pint coffee ice cream

¼ cup lightly toasted chopped pecans

To make the fudge sauce, in a saucepan, combine the cream, butter, corn syrup, and powdered sugar. Set the pan over medium-low heat and heat, stirring with a wooden spatula until the butter melts and the sugar dissolves, about 3 minutes. Add the chocolate and stir until melted, about 2 minutes. Remove from the heat. Stir in the vanilla and let cool until lukewarm before using.

To make the whipped cream, in a large bowl, using an electric mixer, beat the cream, granulated sugar, and vanilla on low speed until the cream begins to thicken and no longer splatters, about 2 minutes. Raise the speed to medium-high and beat until the cream forms soft peaks that fall to one side when the beaters are lifted (turn off the mixer first!), about 3 minutes.

Place the chocolate wafer cookies in a heavy-duty zippered plastic bag and seal shut. Using a rolling pin, roll over the cookies in the bag until coarsely crushed.

Have ready four 12-ounce Mason jars or tall drinking glasses. Spoon about 2 tablespoons of the crushed cookies into each glass, then top each with a scoop of the ice cream, a spoonful of the fudge sauce, and a dollop of the whipped cream. Repeat the layers a second time, reserving some of the crushed cookies to sprinkle with the pecans on top. (Cover and refrigerate any remaining fudge sauce for up to 1 week.) Serve right away, or cover and freeze for up to 4 hours.

Vanilla Ice Cream

Make your own ice cream at home in just a few minutes with this simple recipe, then vary it with your favorite add-ins. Creativity can come into play when serving, too. Try ice cream sandwiches (page 104) or serve scoops atop soda for fun floats (page 99).

MAKES 1 PINT

2 cups cold heavy cream

1 cup cold whole milk

¾ cup sugar, preferably superfine

1 tablespoon vanilla extract

In a large bowl, whisk together the cream and milk. Add the sugar and whisk until completely dissolved, 3 to 4 minutes. Stir in the vanilla. Cover the bowl with plastic wrap and refrigerate for at least 3 hours or up to 24 hours.

Pour the ice cream base into an ice cream maker and freeze according to the manufacturer's instructions. Transfer the ice cream to a freezer-safe container, cover, and freeze until firm, at least 3 hours or up to 3 days.

Variations

Mint Chocolate Chip: Substitute 1½ teaspoons peppermint extract for the vanilla, and add 2 drops green food coloring with the extract, if desired. Add ¾ cup semisweet chocolate chips to the ice cream maker during the last 5 minutes of freezing time.

Cookie Crumble: Add ¾ cup coarsely chopped Oreos or brownies to the ice cream maker during the last 5 minutes of freezing time.

Very Berry: Reduce the vanilla extract to 1 teaspoon. Add 1 cup strawberries, hulled and coarsely chopped, or ripe blackberries to the ice cream maker during the last minute of freezing time.

Coffee: Add 1 cup chilled brewed strong coffee with the cream and milk.

Strawberry Shake

A thick, icy-cold milkshake is about the best way to enjoy a hot summer day. Give the shake some extra flair with whipped cream and a heavy dose of sprinkles, a chocolate-dipped rim, or cut strawberries in the glass or on the rim.

MAKES 2 SHAKES

8 scoops (about 3 cups) strawberry ice cream

½ cup milk

Whipped cream (page 84), for serving

Rainbow sprinkles, for garnish

In a blender, combine the ice cream and milk. Process until well blended. Divide among 2 tall glasses, top with whipped cream, and sprinkle with sprinkles. Add a straw to each glass and serve right away.

Variations

Marshmallow Bubbles: Cut 6 large marshmallows in half. Before filling each glass, stick the cut side of each marshmallow firmly against the inside of the glasses, distributing them evenly. Divide the shake between the glasses.

Sprinkle-Coated Chocolate Rim: Place 1 cup white chocolate chips in a small microwave-safe bowl. Microwave on high for 30 seconds, stir, then microwave at 20-second intervals, stirring at each interval, just until melted and smooth. Spread 2 tablespoons rainbow sprinkles on a saucer. Dip the rim of each glass into the chocolate, then into the sprinkles. Refrigerate the glasses until set, about 10 minutes. Divide the shake between the glasses.

Strawberry Crown: Cut 6 hulled strawberries in half. Press the cut side of each strawberry along the bottom inside edge of each glass, using 6 strawberry halves per glass. Divide the shake between the glasses.

Raspberry Fool

Swirling raspberry purée into whipped cream produces a lovely pink color and fruity flavor, although you can swap in any of your favorite berries with equally delicious results. Whip the cream to stiff peaks so it keeps its volume when you fold in the purée.

MAKES 8 SERVINGS

2 cups raspberries

2 cups cold heavy cream

¼ cup powdered sugar

1 teaspoon vanilla extract

In a food processor or blender, purée the raspberries until smooth. Using a rubber spatula, press the purée through a fine-mesh sieve into a small bowl. Discard the seeds.

In a large bowl, using an electric mixer, beat the cream, powdered sugar, and vanilla on medium-high speed until stiff peaks form when the beaters are lifted (turn off the mixer first!), about 4 minutes.

Using the rubber spatula, gently fold the raspberry purée into the whipped cream. Divide the raspberry fool evenly among 8 glass cups or bowls and serve right away.

Mermaid Pops

Melted white chocolate swirled with ribbons of pink, blue, and purple creates a deep sea–colored coating for vanilla ice cream pops. Making them can be a bit messy, but working in batches will help keep things clean and make the process more manageable.

MAKES 16 POPS

1 pint Vanilla Ice Cream, homemade (page 87) or purchased

16 ice pop sticks

12 ounces white chocolate chips

3 tablespoons coconut oil, melted, plus more as needed

Pink, blue, and purple food coloring

Edible glitter, sprinkles, and/or sanding sugar for decorating (optional)

Line a baking sheet with parchment paper. Using a small ice cream scoop, scoop out 16 balls of the ice cream and place them on the prepared baking sheet. Insert an ice pop stick into each ball. Freeze for 1 hour.

Put half of the white chocolate in a microwave-safe glass bowl. Microwave the chocolate on high in 30-second intervals, stirring at each interval, until melted and smooth. Add 1½ tablespoons of the coconut oil and stir to combine. Transfer about 1 tablespoon of the melted chocolate to each of three small bowls. Add 1 drop of food coloring to each bowl (1 color per bowl) and stir to combine. Use a spoon to drizzle some of each colored chocolate into the bowl of white chocolate. Using a toothpick, briefly swirl the colors together.

Line a cookie sheet with parchment paper, then set a wire cooling rack on top. Working quickly, transfer half of the frozen pops to the wire rack. Pour the swirled glaze evenly over the tops of the pops. Top with sprinkles and/or sanding sugar, if you like. Immediately return the glazed pops to the baking sheet in the freezer.

Repeat the process to glaze the remaining ice pops. Transfer the glazed ice pops to the freezer until set, about 10 minutes. Serve straight from the freezer.

Pineapple Whip

Pineapple is naturally fibrous, so when blended it develops a nice, fluffy texture that makes it perfect for this fruity whip. Prepared with nut milk and agave or maple syrup, this dessert is both vegan and dairy-free. A citrus cup (page 118) makes a fun bowl.

MAKES 4 SERVINGS

1 lb frozen diced pineapple

1¼ cups nut milk, such as macadamia, cashew, or almond

1 tablespoon agave syrup, honey, or maple syrup

Rainbow sprinkles for serving

 In a high-speed blender, combine the pineapple, nut milk, and agave syrup. Process until very smooth, about 3 minutes.

Fit a piping bag with a ½-inch plain tip or snip the corner from a large, heavy-duty zippered bag. Place the bag tip-end down in a glass and carefully spoon the pineapple whip into the bag, leaving about 2 inches free at the top. Gently twist or seal the bag closed. Divide the pineapple whip among 4 serving bowls, piping the whip around the edge of each bowl toward the center. Sprinkle with rainbow sprinkles. Serve right away, or place the bowls in the freezer for up to 2 hours before serving.

Variation

Pineapple Ice Pops: Make the pineapple whip as directed. Spoon the pineapple mixture into four 3-oz ice pop molds, dividing it evenly, and freeze until firm, at least 1 hour.

Cool ideas

Whether you're staying cool with summer snowballs (page 119) or ice cream floats featuring your favorite soda, use your imagination when it comes to dreaming up delicious combos.

Sprinkle-Dipped Bonbons

Make these chocolate-coated ice cream balls when you have a free moment. Store them in a covered container in the freezer to snack on when you want a special treat. Vanilla ice cream is a bonbon classic, but you can use any of your favorite flavors (page 87).

MAKES 25 TO 35 BONBONS

1 pint ice cream, homemade (page 87) or purchased

1 (12-ounce) bag semisweet chocolate chips

2 tablespoons coconut oil or vegetable shortening

¼ cup rainbow sprinkles or chocolate jimmies

Place a baking sheet in the freezer until cold, about 20 minutes.

Remove the baking sheet from the freezer. Using a small ice cream scoop, cookie batter scoop, or melon baller, scoop out small balls of the ice cream and place them on the chilled baking sheet. Cover with plastic wrap and freeze until very cold, 6 to 8 hours.

In a microwave-safe bowl, combine the chocolate chips and oil. Microwave on high power, stirring every 20 seconds, just until the mixture is melted and smooth. Let cool for 5 to 7 minutes.

Put the sprinkles in a small bowl. Using a wooden skewer and a fork and working quickly, skewer an ice cream ball, dip it into the chocolate to cover it completely, then dip the bonbon into the sprinkles, covering it about halfway. Use the fork to push the bonbon from the skewer onto the cold baking sheet. Continue to make the remaining bonbons, spacing them slightly apart on the baking sheet. Freeze until the ice cream is solid and the chocolate is set before serving, at least 2 hours,, or transfer to a large covered container and freeze for up to 2 weeks.

Chocolate-Dipped Frozen Bananas

Because bananas are dense and moist, they're an ideal choice for freezing. Dipped in chocolate, they become an amazing dessert. Use halved bananas as instructed here, or slice the bananas, then dip the slices in chocolate and freeze to create bite-sized treats.

MAKES 4 SERVINGS

2 bananas

4 wooden ice pop sticks

1 cup (about 6 ounces) semisweet chocolate chips

1 tablespoon coconut oil or solid vegetable shortening

About 2 tablespoons finely chopped nuts (any kind) or cacao nibs, toasted shredded coconut, or chopped dehydrated fruit (such as strawberries, raspberries, or pineapple) for sprinkling

Line a baking sheet with parchment paper.

Peel the bananas. Cut off the ends of the bananas and then cut the bananas in half crosswise. Insert an ice pop stick into the cut end of each banana half, pushing in halfway. Place them on the prepared baking sheet and freeze for 30 minutes.

In a microwave-safe bowl, combine the chocolate chips and oil. Microwave on high power, stirring every 20 seconds, just until the mixture is melted and smooth. Let cool for 5 to 7 minutes.

Remove the bananas from the freezer. One at a time, carefully dip the bananas in the chocolate, then return to the baking sheet. Sprinkle with the chopped nuts, cacao nibs, coconut, or dehydrated fruit. Place each banana on the baking sheet and freeze for 30 minutes before serving.

Ice Cream Float

Who doesn't love a fizzy, creamy float? Root beer and vanilla ice cream is the classic pairing, but there are tons of variations. Try some of the options here, or experiment with your own. When in doubt, serve your favorite soda with a scoop of vanilla.

MAKES 2 FLOATS

1 scoop Vanilla
Ice Cream, homemade
(page 87) or purchased

1 can chilled soda,
such as root beer,
cola, orange crush,
or cherry soda

Whipped cream
(page 84) for serving

Sprinkles such as
rainbow sprinkles,
sugar sprinkles, fruity
pebbles cereal, or
crushed dehydrated
fruit, for garnish

 Place 1 scoop of ice cream into a tall glass. Slowly pour in the chilled soda. Top with whipped cream and sprinkles, then serve.

Variations

Raspberry-Orange: Place 1 scoop of vanilla ice cream and 1 scoop of orange sorbet into each glass. Slowly pour in raspberry soda. Top with whipped cream and sprinkles.

Purple Cow: Place 1 scoop of vanilla ice cream in each glass. Slowly pour in grape soda. Top with whipped cream.

Apple Cider: Drizzle 2 tablespoons caramel sauce around the inside of each glass. Add 1 scoop of vanilla ice cream, then slowly fill the glass with sparkling apple cider. Top with whipped cream drizzled with more caramel.

Double Berry: Drizzle 1 tablespoon boysenberry syrup around the inside of each glass. Add 1 scoop of vanilla ice cream, then slowly fill the glass with berry-flavored selter water or blackberry soda. Top with whipped cream and a sprinkling of fresh blackberries.

Orange & Vanilla Parfaits

Cara Cara or blood oranges will lend the deepest hue to this simple sherbet, though Valencia or navel oranges also work well. Whatever variety you use, choose thin-skinned oranges that are heavy for their size to extract the most juice.

MAKES 4 PARFAITS

ORANGE SHERBET

2 cups orange juice (from 4 to 6 oranges)

¼ cup sugar

1 cup whole milk

About 1⅓ cups vanilla ice cream, purchased or homemade (page 87)

Strips of orange peel or orange slices for garnish (optional)

To make the orange sherbet, in a bowl, stir together the orange juice and sugar until the sugar dissolves. Strain the mixture through a fine-mesh sieve into a nonaluminum bowl. Pour the milk into another bowl. Cover both bowls with plastic wrap and refrigerate until very cold, at least 3 hours or up to 8 hours.

Pour the milk into the bowl with the orange juice and stir until blended. Pour the sherbet base into an ice cream maker and freeze according to the manufacturer's instructions. Transfer the sherbet to a freezer-safe container, cover, and freeze until firm, at least 3 hours or up to 3 days.

To make the parfaits, scoop a regular-size scoop (about ⅓ cup) of orange sherbet into each of 4 parfait glasses. Top each with a scoop of vanilla ice cream, then another scoop of orange sherbet. (Cover and freeze any remaining sherbet for another use.) Garnish each glass with a strip of orange peel or an orange slice, if you like, and serve.

Watermelon Granita

This granita tastes like pure, frozen watermelon. Even a small amount of undissolved sugar in the syrup can cause the granita to be grainy, so watch carefully and don't remove the syrup from the heat too soon.

MAKES ABOUT 3½ CUPS

½ cup sugar

½ cup white grape juice or water

1 small seedless watermelon, about 1 pound, well chilled

1 tablespoon lemon juice

In a small saucepan, stir together the sugar and white grape juice. Set the pan over medium-high heat and bring to a boil, stirring once or twice, 3 to 4 minutes. Boil the syrup, stirring frequently, until it is clear and there are no visible grains of sugar, 1 to 2 minutes. Remove from the heat and pour the syrup into a heatproof bowl. Let cool, then cover the bowl with plastic wrap and refrigerate until very cold, about 1 hour.

Ask an adult to help you cut the watermelon in half. Scoop the flesh from the watermelon and cut into chunks, if needed. (You should have about 4 cups.) Transfer the watermelon to a blender or food processor. Add the sugar syrup and lemon juice and purée until smooth, about 30 seconds.

Pour the watermelon purée into a shallow 3-quart metal pan, such as a 9-by-13-inch baking pan. Cover the pan with aluminum foil and freeze until a thin layer of ice forms on the surface and the edges begin to harden about ½ inch in from the sides, about 1 hour.

Remove the pan from the freezer and remove the foil. Using a sturdy dinner fork, run the tines across the surface of the granita, breaking up any frozen areas into small pieces, then mix those pieces back into the liquid. Cover the pan and freeze again for about 30 minutes, then repeat the scraping and mixing procedure. Do this 3 or 4 more times until the granita is icy and grainy throughout, about 2½ hours total. Serve right away or freeze for up to 1 day. Granita is at its best if served within 4 hours of freezing.

Cantaloupe Sorbet

A simple but magical combination of fruit and sugar, sorbet is an especially refreshing treat. The recipe calls for cantaloupe, one of summer's most recognizable melons, but try any of your favorite varieties, such as honeydew, Crenshaw, Canary, or watermelon.

MAKES ABOUT 1 QUART

1 cantaloupe, about
2 pounds

½ cup sugar

2 tablespoons light
corn syrup

Cut the cantaloupe in half and remove the seeds with a spoon. Place the halves, cut side down, on the cutting board and cut into slices. Using a small, sharp knife, cut along the rind to remove it from each slice, then cut the melon into cubes.

Transfer the melon cubes to a food processor or blender. Purée until smooth. (You should have about 2⅓ cups purée.) Transfer the purée to a bowl and add the sugar and corn syrup. Stir until the sugar dissolves, about 2 minutes. Cover the bowl with plastic wrap and refrigerate until cold, about 2 hours.

Pour the sorbet base into an ice cream maker and freeze according to the manufacturer's instructions. Transfer the sorbet to a freezer-safe container, cover, and freeze until firm, at least 4 hours or up to 3 days.

Variation

Cantaloupe Sorbet Pops: Decrease the amount of each ingredient by half, using ½ cantaloupe, ¼ cup sugar, and 1 tablespoon light corn syrup. Purée as directed, then stir in the sugar and corn syrup until dissolved. Spoon the mixture into six 2-oz ice pop molds, dividing it evenly. Freeze until firm, at least 3 hours or up to overnight.

Ice Cream Sandwiches

You'll have a blast making these sandwiches with your friends. Use store-bought cookies and ice cream or make your own (page 87). Slightly underbake the cookies or select ones that are chewy to prevent the ice cream from oozing out when you take a bite.

MAKES ABOUT 6 SANDWICHES

1 pint ice cream, purchased or homemade (page 87)

1 cup semi-sweet chocolate chips

1 tablespoon coconut oil or solid vegetable shortening

12 3-inch cookies (see note)

Chocolate and rainbow sprinkles for decorating

Remove the ice cream from the freezer and let stand at room temperature until softened slightly, about 10 minutes. Line a cookie sheet with parchment paper.

Meanwhile, in a microwave-safe bowl, combine the chocolate chips and oil. Microwave on high power, stirring every 20 seconds, just until the mixture is melted and smooth. Let cool for 5 to 7 minutes.

Place a scoop of softened ice cream on the underside of each of 6 cookies, dividing the ice cream evenly. Top each scoop with another cookie, underside down. Press the cookies together gently until the ice cream reaches the edge of the cookies. Working with 1 sandwich at a time, dip a sandwich into the chocolate, covering it about halfway, then sprinkle with sprinkles.

Place the sandwiches on the prepared baking sheet and freeze until set, about 10 minutes. Serve right away, or transfer to a covered container and freeze for up to 3 days.

Serving tip
Try any of your favorite cookies to make these cool treats. Oatmeal (page 38), chocolate (page 39), and plain snickerdoodles (page 36) are all good options.

Fruit Slushies

This bag-shaking technique for making fruit slushies takes some stamina, but is well worth the effort. Partner with a friend to make different flavors, then layer them one at a time in each glass like the orange and strawberry juice slushies pictured here.

MAKES 1 SERVING

3 cups ice cubes

1 tablespoon salt

1 cup fruit juice

Place the ice in a gallon-size heavy-duty zippered plastic bag. Sprinkle the salt over the ice and seal the bag shut. Using your hands, massage the bag to mix well. Pour the fruit juice into a quart-size heavy-duty zippered plastic bag and seal shut. Put the small bag of juice into the large bag of ice, surrounding the juice bag as much as possible with the ice. Shake vigorously (you should get some exercise during this step!) until the juice is slushy, 3 to 5 minutes. Pour the slushy into a glass and serve.

Celebration Pops

These red, white, and blue pops are a cool way to celebrate on Independence Day. To make sure the colorful layers are distinct, freeze each new flavor layer in the ice pops molds until it has a slushy consistency before adding the next one.

MAKES 6 TO 8 POPS

1 teaspoon finely grated lemon zest

½ cup lemon juice

½ cup plus 2 tablespoons superfine sugar

Pinch of salt

1½ cups water

Red and blue food coloring

In a pitcher, combine the lemon zest and juice, superfine sugar, and salt. Add the water and stir to dissolve the sugar. Pour about one-third of the lemonade into a smaller pitcher and half of the remaining lemonade into a third pitcher.

Stir 3 drops of red food coloring into the first pitcher, stir 3 drops of blue food coloring into the second pitcher, and leave the lemonade in the third pitcher uncolored.

Fill 6 to 8 ice pop molds one-third of the way with the red lemonade. Freeze until partially frozen, about 1 hour. Pour the uncolored lemonade into the molds, dividing it evenly over the red layer. If using ice pop sticks, insert them at this point. Freeze until partially frozen, about 1 hour.

Pour the blue lemonade over the uncolored layer, dividing it evenly. Freeze until solid, at least 3 hours or up to 3 days.

Before serving, run the molds under hot water for a few seconds to release the pops, then serve.

Chocolate Pudding Pops

Do you love chocolate but it's too hot to bake? Try these creamy, chocolaty, icy pops for a yummy treat. To cool the chocolate mixture quickly, nestle the pan in a bowl of ice water and stir until the mixture reaches room temperature, then fill the molds.

MAKES 8 TO 10 POPS

1¼ cups whole milk

1 cup heavy cream

2 tablespoons unsweetened cocoa powder

1 teaspoon vanilla extract

Pinch of salt

4 ounces bittersweet or semisweet chocolate, chopped

2 tablespoons sugar

In a saucepan, combine the milk, cream, cocoa powder, vanilla, and salt. Set the pan over medium heat and bring to a simmer, whisking to dissolve the cocoa. Add the chocolate and stir until dissolved, then stir in the sugar. Place the saucepan in a large bowl of ice water to help it cool quickly. Let the chocolate mixture cool completely, stirring occasionally.

Pour the cocoa mixture into a small pitcher or glass measuring cup. Divide the mixture evenly among 8 to 10 ice pop molds. Cover and freeze until solid, at least 4 hours or up to 3 days. If using ice pop sticks, insert them into the molds when the pops are partially frozen, after about 1 hour, then continue to freeze until solid, at least 3 more hours.

Before serving, run the molds under hot water for a few seconds to release the pops, then serve.

Coconut-Mango-Strawberry Pops

Although these colorful, dairy-free pops are the perfect treat on a hot summer day, they're delicious any time of year! Serve them with your other ice pop favorites, such as the Yogurt Swirl Ice Pops (page 112) and Pineapple Ice Pops (page 92) pictured here.

MAKES 6 POPS

1 (13.5-fluid-ounce) can full-fat coconut milk

1 cup frozen mango chunks

2 tablespoons maple syrup, plus more if needed

1 cup frozen strawberries or blueberries

¼ cup water, plus more if needed

6 ice pop sticks

In a blender or food processor, combine the coconut milk, mango, and maple syrup. Blend until smooth. Taste and add more maple syrup if the mixture needs to be sweeter. Pour the mixture into a small pitcher or glass measuring cup.

Rinse the blender and add the strawberries and water. Blend until a smooth purée forms, adding more water, 1 tablespoon at a time, if needed. Pour the mixture into another small pitcher or glass measuring cup.

Pour the strawberry mixture into 3 of the ice pop molds, using about half of the mixture and filling the molds halfway. Pour the mango mixture into the remaining 3 ice pop molds, using about half of the mixture and filling the molds halfway. Freeze until partially frozen, about 30 minutes. Pour the remaining fruit mixtures over the partially frozen pops, dividing the mixtures evenly and alternating the flavors. If using ice pop sticks, insert them at this point. Freeze until solid, 3 to 4 hours.

Before serving, run the molds under hot water for a few seconds to release the pops, then serve.

Berry-Yogurt Swirl Ice Pops

Puréed berries are a delicious partner to vanilla yogurt in these refreshing pops, but feel free to experiment with any of your own favorite fruit additions. Try halved and pitted cherries, or diced peaches, apricots, plums, kiwi fruit, or mango.

MAKES 12 TO 14 ICE POPS

2½ cups berries (such as strawberries, blueberries, or blackberries), hulled and cut in half

2 tablespoons superfine sugar

1 teaspoon lemon juice

Pinch of salt

1½ cups vanilla whole-milk yogurt

12 to 14 ice pop sticks

 In a blender or food processor, combine the strawberries, sugar, lemon juice, and salt. Process until completely smooth.

Place 2 tablespoons of the yogurt in each ice pop mold. Top each with 2 tablespoons of the berry mixture. Continue layering the yogurt and berry mixture in the molds until the molds are full. Dip a knife into each mold and make a few figure-eight motions to swirl the flavors together. Cover and freeze until solid, at least 4 hours or up to 3 days. If using ice pop sticks, insert them into the molds when the pops are partially frozen, after about 1 hour, then continue to freeze until solid, about 3 hours.

Before serving, run the molds under hot water for a few seconds to release the pops, then serve.

Fruity Ice Pops

Sweet fruit mixtures frozen into portable pops are about the best way to stay cool when the temperature outside is hot. Try these summery combinations or experiment with your own. A little bit of sugar adds sweetness and a smooth texture.

MAKES 6 TO 10 POPS

½ cup sugar

2 strips lime zest

½ cup water

4 cups diced
honeydew melon

Lime juice, to taste

8 ice pop sticks

Lime & Honeydew Melon In a small saucepan, combine the sugar, lime zest, and water. Set the pan over medium-high heat and bring to a boil, stirring often, until the sugar dissolves, 3–4 minutes. Let cool. Remove the zest and discard. Transfer the sugar syrup to a blender and add the melon. Process until smooth. Add lime juice to taste. Pour the melon mixture into a small pitcher or glass measuring cup. Divide the melon mixture evenly among 8 ice pop molds. Cover and freeze until solid, at least 4 hours or up to 3 days. If using ice pop sticks, insert them into the molds when the pops are partially frozen, after about 1 hour, then continue to freeze until solid, at least 3 more hours.

1 cup orange juice

5 tablespoons honey

Pinch of salt

¼ cup plus
2 tablespoons water

3 black plums, halved,
pitted, and cut into wedges

6 to 8 ice pop sticks

Plum & Orange In a small pitcher or glass measuring cup, stir together the orange juice, honey, and salt. Add the water and stir to combine. Fill 6 to 8 ice pop molds about halfway with the orange juice mixture, add a few plum wedges to each mold, and freeze until partially frozen, about 1 hour. Add the remaining juice mixture and plums to the molds. If using ice pop sticks, insert them at this point and continue to freeze until solid, at least 4 hours or up to 3 days.

Serving tip
To make unmolding the pops a cinch, run the bottom of the frozen ice pop molds under warm running water, then pull the pops free.

4 cups raspberries

¼ cup plus 1 tbsp superfine sugar

¼ cup fresh peppermint leaves

Pinch of salt

¼ cup water

8 to 10 ice pop sticks

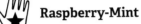

Raspberry-Mint
In a blender or food processor, combine the raspberries, sugar, peppermint leaves, and salt. Pour in the ¼ cup water. Process until completely smooth. Strain the raspberry mixture through a fine-mesh sieve set over a small pitcher or glass measuring cup. Discard the raspberry seeds and peppermint leaves. Divide the raspberry mixture evenly among 8 to 10 ice pop molds. Cover and freeze until solid, at least 4 hours or up to 3 days. Insert the icepop sticks into the molds when the pops are partially frozen, after about 1 hour, then continue to freeze until solid, at least 3 more hours.

3 ripe peaches, about 1 lb total weight, peeled if desired

¼ cup superfine sugar

1 tablespoon freshly squeezed lemon juice (from 1 lemon)

Pinch of salt

¼ cup water

6 to 8 ice pop sticks

Fresh Peach Cut the peaches in half and remove the pits, then chop the flesh. Place in a blender or food processor. Add the sugar, lemon juice, salt, and the ¼ cup water and process until the mixture is completely smooth. Pour the peach mixture into a small pitcher or glass measuring cup. Divide the peach mixture evenly among 6 to 8 ice pop molds. Cover and freeze until solid, at least 4 hours or up to 3 days. If using ice pop sticks, insert them into the molds when the pops are partially frozen, after about 1 hour, then continue to freeze until solid, at least 3 more hours.

Poolside Piña Colada Slushies

Originating in Puerto Rico, this tangy pineapple and rich coconut drink pairs best with a poolside seat, a pair of sunglasses, and a stereo blasting your favorite songs. Be sure to slather on some sunscreen!

MAKES 2 SERVINGS

1 cup ice cubes

3 bananas, peeled and broken into chunks

1 cup frozen pineapple chunks, plus pineapple wedges for garnish (optional)

1 cup whole milk

½ cup pineapple juice

3 tablespoons coconut cream

In a blender, combine the ice cubes, bananas, pineapple, milk, pineapple juice, and coconut cream. Blend until smooth. Divide the slushy between 2 glasses, garnish with pineapple wedges, and serve.

Slushy bling
Garnish your glass with flourish — a skewer of fresh fruit, a wedge of pineapple, or a sprinkling of coconut are all good additions.

Frozen Lemonade in Lemon Cups

Fresh citrus cups make fun bowls for frozen lemonade, though you can swap them for ordinary bowls to save time. For larger citrus cups, try hollowed-out grapefruits or oranges instead of the lemons, adding a spoon and a straw to each one for the lemonade.

MAKES 6 SERVINGS

6 large lemons

1 cup sugar, preferably superfine

5 cups cold water

Cut each lemon crosswise into halves. Juice the lemons into a pitcher. (You should have about 1 cup juice.) Using the tip of a spoon, scrape out any remaining pulp and pith from each lemon half. Cut a thin slice from the rounded bottom halves of each lemon to make them stand upright. Place on a baking sheet (or an empty egg carton) and freeze until solid, about 1 hour.

Add the sugar to the lemon juice and stir until dissolved. Stir in the water.

Fill 2 empty 12-cube ice cube trays with the lemonade and freeze until solid, about 4 hours. Refrigerate the remaining lemonade.

Remove the ice cubes from the tray and transfer to a blender. Pulse until finely chopped. Continue to pulse, adding a little bit of the remaining lemonade to the mixture if needed, until the desired slushy consistency is reached. Scoop the slushy lemonade into the frozen lemon halves and serve right away.

Summer Snowballs

While fruity cereals yield explosively colorful snowballs, other cereals also make a fantastic addition to ice cream. Crushed cinnamon-sugar cereal creates a sweetly spiced snowball, while chocolate cereal makes a bonbon-like snowball—use your imagination!

MAKES 4 TO 6 SERVINGS

1 pint ice cream, purchased or homemade (page 87)

1 cup fruity pebbles cereal

Place a baking sheet in the freezer until cold, about 20 minutes.

Remove the baking sheet from the freezer. Using a small ice cream scoop, cookie batter scoop, or melon baller, scoop out small balls of the ice cream and place them on the chilled baking sheet. Cover with plastic wrap and freeze until firm, about 1 hour.

Pour the cereal into a shallow bowl. Remove the ice cream from the freezer. Working with 1 ball at a time, add the ball to the cereal in the bowl and roll to coat, pressing the cereal onto the ice cream if needed. Eat right away or store in a covered container in the freezer for up to 2 days.

Index

weldon**owen**

1150 Brickyard Cove Road
Richmond, CA 94801
www.weldonowen.com

WELDON OWEN
CEO Raoul Goff
President Kate Jerome
Publisher Roger Shaw
Associate Publisher Amy Marr
Senior Editor Lisa Atwood
Creative Director Chrissy Kwasnik
Photography Art Director & Designer Lisa Berman
Original Design Ali Zeigler

Managing Editor Tarji Rodriguez
Production Manager Binh Au
Imaging Manager Don Hill

Photographer Nicole Hill Gerulat
Food Stylist Carrie Purcell
Wardrobe & Prop Stylists Veronica Olson
Hair & Makeup Kathy Hill

AMERICAN GIRL *SUMMER TREATS*

Conceived and produced by Weldon Owen International

A WELDON OWEN PRODUCTION

Printed and bound in China

First printed in 2020
10 9 8 7 6 5 4 3 2 1

Library of Congress Cataloging in Publication
data is available

ISBN: 978-1-68188-516-2

ACKNOWLEDGMENTS
Weldon Owen wishes to thank the following people for their generous support to help produce this book:
Lisa Chavarria, Aubrey Devin, Linda Jean Erikson, Bronwyn Lane, Eve Lynch, Andrew Meredith,
Alexis Mersel, A'Lissa Olson, Taylor Olson, Elizabeth Parson, and Angelique Strachan.

A VERY SPECIAL THANK YOU TO:
Our models: Nina Fife, Kaelin Lagarde, Jayden Lam, Toni Lopez,
Malyah Phillips, Malia Smith, Jordan Taylor.

Our location: The Fife Family

Collect Them All

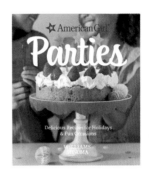

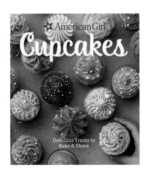